IN HER ROOM

JOAN M. R. JOLIN

To Gregg
For the San Diego
"trip" '84
the Delaware
FAIRYTALES '84

from "Thumper" AKA
Jeannie
THANX

Cover design & layout of text: Steve Daigle
Cover photo: Carol Lou Edwards
Cranberry Tree Press
5060 Tecumseh Rd. E, Suite 173
Windsor, Ontario, Canada, N8T 1C1
Printed in Canada

National Library of Canada Cataloguing in Publication

Jolin, Joan M. R
    In her room / Joan M.R. Jolin.

ISBN 1-894668-10-3

    1. Cancer–Patients–Family relationships. 2. Cancer–Psychological aspects. 3. Bereavement–Psychological aspects. 4. Jolin, Joan M. R.–Diaries. I. Title.

RC280.L9J645 2002   155.9'16   C2002-901951-6

 CRANBERRY TREE PRESS

Acknowledgements

Patricia Conlin, my Creative Writing Workshop 'mate'. A gifted writer, Pat was the first person to read my manuscript. Her astute and thoughtful review took several weeks. She refused any form of payment. She said she felt honoured to be asked to read my journal. She told me to publish 'no matter what'.

Carol Lou Edwards, gardener, artist, photographer, for the gift of her picture of the Azalea gracing the book's cover.

Kelly Walker, for the use of the song 'Paradise' from his newest CD 'All My Life' and for his willingness to let me put my books on his table at the International Palliative Care Conference in June, 2002 in Windsor, Ontario.

Jeannie, my beloved sister, for her unfailing love and encouragement throughout the writing and editing of my journal.

May Sarton, for making the journal a legitimate literary form.

The staff and volunteers at The Hospice of Windsor and Essex County, Inc. for the extraordinary work they do with the people of our community suffering from a life-threatening illness. Most especially to Maggie, June, Rev. Jurrien, the two Heathers, Debbie, Donna, Bill, Christine, Rosemary, Dr. Charmaine Jones, Carole, Jan, Shirley and Armand.

Laurie Smith, my editor, for her green pen pruning out the 'bad' bits. As a teacher with unflinching candor, as well as a supportive mentor, along with Lenore Langs, she was willing to publish my first work of length.

To my darling Guy for reading the manuscript. Guy's love and support sustained me through his own illness and through the fear. I love you.

Joan M. R. Jolin, B.S.W.
Windsor, Ontario
March, 2002

TABLE OF CONTENTS

Acknowledgements vii

Prologue x

Family & Friends xiii

Natalie 1

In Her Room 3

Epilogue 108

Letters 112

About the Author 115

PROLOGUE

In January of 1998, Nathalie, my husband's 22 year old niece, was diagnosed with Non-Hodgkins Lymphoma. Nathalie was one of three children born to Guy's eldest sister, Germaine.

Nathalie was her baby.

Prior to the diagnosis and even at times throughout it, Nathalie was like a beautiful expectant bud inviting love and life to embrace her. As the cancer ravaged her body in its relentless mutation, she became as fragile as the petals of a waning Iceland Poppy. But though her body descended in increasing frailty Nathalie's spirit soared.

She never spoke of death to me, though one night her mother thought she heard her say, "I'm dying. I'm dying." Germaine couldn't be certain that what she'd heard weren't whispers frightened from the darkness of the night.

Until the moment of her death, Germaine and Nathalie were together through doctor and hospital visits, tests, x-rays, a bone marrow transplant at Princess Margaret Hospital in Toronto, blood transfusions, chemotherapy and two brief remissions.

Guy and I knew what was happening but we lived it at a distance. All of that changed when Nathalie became ill again in the fall of '99 when we began to journey with Germaine and Nathalie. Nathalie died on December 23, 1999 at 12:31 a.m.

Behind my eyes, I can see Nathalie coming up the stairs from her bedroom in her parents' split-level home. She was short of breath. She sat on the couch and I sat beside her until she was able to speak. She was clearly in trouble. The cancer had returned with a vengeance. My intuition told me that this time was different. This time Guy and I better get closer or we'd miss a sacred experience. It was the first time I'd allowed myself to consider the possibility that Nathalie might die.

Ironically it was Hallowe'en when I began to record my thoughts and feelings in a journal. I had no idea that I would ever publish. My work sat in a file folder for months gathering dust. Then I was overcome with a sense of urgency that it was my responsibility to publish the journal. It felt that the imperative came from Nathalie herself. I knew Nathalie had something to say about life; something which might help another person cope with their own suffering in a positive way. A way for someone else to find meaning, even joy, from the sorrow which necessarily accompanies our journey from birth to death.

I felt compelled to display in my home a photograph of the collage created by Chantal of dozens of pictures of Nathalie which stood on an easel in the funeral home. I put the photograph in my bathroom with a five day blue candle. The kind of candle burned in Roman Catholic churches. Nathalie would appreciate the irony. There is Hedera Ivy in a diminutive vase given to Guy and I on our 25th wedding anniversary, October 10, 2000, from my dear parish sponsor, Rita. I sometimes nestle flowers in the arms of the Ivy. Every Sunday I light the candle in memory of Nathalie.

FAMILY & FRIENDS

Nathalie 'Nat'
Germaine, Nathalie's mother
Germain 'Gerry', Nathalie's father
Martin 'Marty', Nathalie's brother
Chantal, Nathalie's sister & Darrin, Nathalie's brother-in-law
Claude & Nelly, Nathalie's maternal uncle and aunt
Robert & Huguette, Nathalie's maternal uncle and aunt
Nicole & Jean Guy, Remy, Nathalie's maternal
    aunt, uncle and cousin
Guy, Nathalie's maternal uncle and husband of the author
Micheline, Nathalie's maternal aunt
Pierrette, Nathalie's maternal aunt
Rob, Nathalie's blue-eyed Celt
Charlotte, Andrew, Alex & Katherine,
    Rob's Mom, brothers & sister
Sammi*, a friend of Nathalie's
Jennifer, from Calgary, a friend of Nathalie's
Greg & Janina, the author's son and granddaughter
Lynda, the author's daughter
Courtney & Benjamin, the author's grandchildren
Kenny, the author's former son-in-law
Blake & Debbie, the author's son and daughter-in-law
Matthew and Brandon, the author's
    grandsons, sons of Blake & Debbie

*pseudonyms

IN MEMORY OF
NATALIE, 1975-1999
for Germaine with love and gratitude

IN HER ROOM

October 31, 1999 – Trick or Treat?

"I'm tired, Aunt Joan," she says. "I asked my doctor if I'll have to fight this disease for the rest of my life and she said yes. This changes my view of life as I once envisioned it. Now I'll have to choose a career that will make space for the on again/off again need for chemotherapy, rest and time off work. I'm still not sure what kind of a career THAT will be, given everything I'll need. Perhaps Rob will ask me to marry him and he will take care of me forever." She said this in a shy, somewhat bemused way as if she could just bring herself to begin to entertain the thought.

I could feel my rage roiling like a dark storm as I stifled a gasp. Was the doctor just being diplomatic when she'd answered Nathalie's question so simply and straightforwardly? She wasn't really lying since there was no mention of the potential length of Nat's life. Perhaps a few months? But I must remember Nat's not looking at her life in this way – in the way I am – she's looking at it in terms of years between remissions. Five? Twenty? More?

"But you know, Aunt Joan, I've only been given four or five months – so far – between remissions."

The question, how long this time, hung in the air like Spanish moss from a Georgia shade tree.

I've grown to love this young woman. I want to scream at the fates for their cruelty. For shortening the life of the bud before it has the chance to become a full-blown rose.

Not that she hasn't already made a difference in my life. I remember our talk while walking along the street in Huntsville, returning to the motel from the restaurant after dinner. We were on our way to visit Guy's brother, Claude, on the occasion of his 25th wedding anniversary. It was the first time I'd really talked with Nathalie. I was stunned by her wisdom. At age 18 she spoke of topics like life-after-death, near death experience, out-of-body experience and reincarnation.

She was curious and open to all of life's possibilities.

I felt her innate decency. She was a thoroughly modern girl mingled with a fragrance of sweet old-fashionedness. She enjoyed going to bars. She liked men, especially Rob, since he's THE one.

Nathalie was irreverent at times and deeply spiritual at others. She could be wonderfully 'wild and crazy' wearing her long dark wig when she went out to cover her baldness. Her garish nail polish. Rings on every finger and multiple earrings, including the one high up on her right ear, that my husband, Guy, wiggled with affection every time he greeted her.

I loved her baldness. It made her so vulnerable – so exposed. I wanted to wrap her in my arms so no one would ever hurt her again.

I think God is greedy. He wants to surround Himself with beautiful, funny people to stave off His sorrow at the mess we've made of His world.

Even though I know the futility of the question I can't help wanting to scream, Why? Why Nathalie? Why now? Why not someone old who's already had a chance? Why someone with such potential to bring beauty into the world? Why a young woman who runs into life drinking every moment of joy from it? Why take her when You leave others who seem so useless; an added burden to society; of no benefit to anyone, including themselves? People who beg God every day to take them – now.

Why her and not me?

That's the mystery of life and death, isn't it? I have no control over anything except my response to what it is that life presents to me. I wonder to myself, would I appreciate Nathalie so much as I do if I knew she'd be around for years and years? Does the shortening of her time with us make her presence all the more poignant and precious, like the lily which blooms for one glorious day before fading and dying? Like the butterfly which after a time sleeping in a chrysalis emerges in all its beauty to live a life known for its brevity?

I look into her sweet face wondering how many more

times I'll be privileged to see her smile or touch her hand and kiss her gently on the cheek or buy her a tiny toy lamb named Tumbles. And that uncertainty and unknowing make my time with her filled with gratitude that she's in my life at all.

I remember again the truth I'd rather forget. When one loves one invites the pain of separation. It's true, too, that the love is worth the pain. I can hear Debra Winger's character, Joy, saying words to this effect to Anthony Hopkins' character, C. S. Lewis in the film, "Shadowlands". If I don't open my heart to Nathalie, being willing to walk with her through whatever is before her, I will be the poorer for it.

November 6, 1999

Nathalie has been moved to a private room. Guy and I saw her yesterday at noon hour. She was being given transfusions of blood and platelets, an IV with saline and oxygen. Her pain must have been intense. Germaine is continually rubbing her back – right around where her kidneys are – and Nathalie won't let anyone take over. She says only her Mom knows how to 'get it right'. We could see this is hard on Germaine. How will she cope in the days ahead as Nathalie requires more care and attention? She wants her mother to stay overnight and so a cot was being provided for Germaine to sleep on right in the room beside Nathalie's bed.

Nathalie doesn't want to talk to the Hospice nurse making it nearly impossible to find a 'good' level of pain control. Her unwillingness to work with the Hospice makes it difficult for Germaine to get some relief from her caregiver's role. Nathalie is like a little child once more wanting only her Mama for comfort. I've heard it said that grown men cry out for their mothers in times of sorrow especially in the stillness of the prison night.

Guy is worried for his sister and so am I.

Hospice volunteers would be invaluable right now. I wish Germaine would contact them and take advantage of their wonderful help.

I endeavour to offer Germaine a sounding board as I'm

hopeless when it comes to sitting quietly with someone who is very ill. My nature seems unable to provide the needed peace. I'm all fire. Sagittarius. I try not to beat myself up for being who I am. I endeavour to find ways of offering help and support by being present with her and listening. Skills pruned from fifteen years as a psychotherapist. Not an easy task for someone as talkative as I am.

On the other hand, Guy is the perfect companion for someone who is very ill. He will sit quietly beside their bed, his wonderful strong heart beating slowly and surely. A man not given to long conversations he brings a calm, serene presence to bear that comforts and consoles like his sun sign, Scorpio, his way cooling as a soft rain after a long, hot, dry summer.

I have offered Germaine my help nearly every time I've seen her. Not once has she taken me up on my offer. When her neighbour, Pat, offered her help Germaine was able to ask her for some of her delicious cabbage rolls. I'm not sure why Germaine's reluctant to accept my help. I've thought about it quite a bit even getting angry on more than one occasion. Is it too hard for her because I'm not her sister? Because I don't speak French? I find it hard to know what to do without being pushy or sticking my nose in where it's not wanted. I would be willing to help her with meals, cooking, housecleaning, running errands if she wanted me to but I get the sense she doesn't want me to know her business and when someone lets you do these things you do get to know the other person's business.

My mother used to say when in doubt, do nothing, so I try to leave it with God trusting He'll show me what to do.

Guy's eldest brother, Claude, will be coming down in a week or two picking up their youngest sister, Pierrette, in Toronto along the way. He will be bringing the mailbox and house sign with 'The Jolins' painted on it that his wife, Nelly, painted for us. It is our 25th wedding anniversary gift – a year early! What a delightful surprise.

The doctor has told Germaine – not Nathalie – that he will do his best to keep her alive until Christmas. He's given her two to six months, Germaine said. Nathalie will be given a mild chemotherapy – is there such a thing? – for five days after which she can return home. To die there? I hope Germaine will ask for help when this happens as she will be Nathalie's primary caregiver and 'on call' 24 hours a day. Nathalie sleeps on the lower level of their split-level home. This means Germaine will have to run up and down the stairs. Nathalie has a bell that she rings when she wants or needs anything.

Germaine gets angry about the disarray in the house. She feels she has enough to do looking after Nathalie without having to cope with cooking meals and cleaning. I wonder if she's considered having someone come in say once a week to do the housekeeping chores? I wish I could be doing these things to help. I ask myself over and over why it is I resist offering?

No results from the lung biopsy, but Nathalie's coughing up blood.

We ran into a friend of Guy's from work and his wife. I love hearing Jim* speak. His voice has a soft Scottish burr. A friend of Jim's, a man of 51 years of age, was in the room next to Nat with exactly the same disease. He'd had a ten month remission and is now facing a bone marrow transplant.

Jim is such fun, giving me a big hug when we met. The first time he's ever done that. We asked about the fish we'd given him from the water garden at our old house. We couldn't take them with us to our new one. He grimaced saying he couldn't bring himself to tell us that all of them had died. It seems that one day he went to play golf and was gone all day with his wife. When they came home the pump hadn't stopped running that entire time. The pond was completely empty and over 100 fish, including his many koi and all of the ones we gave him, lay dead on the pond's bottom. Even 'Eugene", the algae eater Guy had named and loved. "Eugene" was a lovely black colour quite unique in the shop where we'd found him. He was a handsome 'fellow', too, unless you looked closely at his mouth!

Speaking about his friend and Nathalie, Jim shared that he didn't believe in a God who permitted such suffering and he couldn't understand when others did. I often have negative thoughts about God especially when I think of God as male though, of course, I know that God is a loving spirit. I'm not sure I'd want to survive without my faith. I can talk to Him and believe I'm being heard even though I don't 'hear' a voice. It IS hard to believe in something you can't see but I've felt His love for me and my family enough to know He exists and He loves each one of us no matter who we are or what we've done.

November 7, 1999

I must remember to ask Germaine if the doctor told her Nathalie had two to six months to live or simply said 'two to six'? Did Germaine add the months without realizing that when the doctor said he'd do his best to keep her alive until Christmas that he actually meant two to six weeks? Did I hear Germaine wrong? Did I want to hear months?

Guy and I are planning to go to the hospital later today. He'll try to arrange to be alone with Nathalie so Germaine and I can spend some time together. Then I'll ask her our question. It's important that it be asked in spite of the difficulty. After all, weeks and months are vastly different. It is possible that Nathalie might not even survive the mild chemotherapy in her weakened state.

I talked to my sister, Jeannie, yesterday. It always helps. Her years as a Palliative Care volunteer with the dying and most recently with people with AIDS has garnered her a wide breadth of skill. She said that we don't know how we are meant to be helpful until after the fact. We must simply stay open to whatever comes and flow with it. I know for now that I must not offer to do anything for Germaine at home unless she's there with me. I would be quite comfortable doing whatever she asked of me. This isn't likely to happen as she spends most of the day and night at the hospital. I feel she's made it abundantly clear that for whatever reason she doesn't want my help or is unable to ask for it.

I want to help.

I had thought I'd say something to her sisters about coming

down for her but realize this is my issue and that I'm meant to keep my mouth shut. I feel very much that I need to step carefully since I'm not Germaine's sister and at times like this it is our relationships with our immediate family which are of primary importance.

It seems clearer to me now why I can't think of anything to do when Guy's in Quebec City over the holidays with Jam des Neiges. I'm exactly where I'm meant to be. I'm here for Germaine as much as she needs me to be.

November 8, 1999

Guy and I went to the hospital yesterday around noon. Germaine had just left 15 minutes before we arrived to go home and rest. Gerry was with Nathalie who appeared to be sleeping more peacefully.

Germaine had gotten just four hours sleep during the night and Gerry had told her to take her time, that he didn't mind sitting quietly with Nathalie. He was doing crossword puzzles when we arrived, sitting in the chair at the end of the bed.

Guy offered to sit with Nathalie so Gerry could have a break. He and I went into the Cancer Centre's Resource Library. They have quite a few books that can be borrowed for two weeks. I found a pamphlet about caring for a cancer patient at home. I showed it to Gerry and he was reading it later when Guy and I left.

As Gerry and I sat together he talked about leaving Windsor when he retired and moving near the water so he could have a boat and go fishing. He talked a lot about his pension, possibly buying an RV and travelling to Florida in the cold weather and to a place he might buy up near North Bay. He definitely didn't want to go back to Quebec. He said it was too cold in the winter time with too much snow to shovel and there was too much rain in the summer. The possibility of returning to the former city was mentioned as well as moving closer to his elder daughter, Chantal, who lives out-of-town. But of the utmost importance was his love of fishing and being near water. He said he fished a lot as a young man and missed it.

These moments in life are so precious and increasingly rare. Moments when two people sit together sharing their thoughts and feelings in a gentle, caring way. These happenings which remind us of our interdependence are sweeter because of their spontaneity. I was granted a gift from Gerry. An opportunity to see him with entirely different eyes and from, until then, a hidden place. Our relationship changed for me from that moment. I began to glimpse a depth in him I'd not been permitted to see and hadn't bothered taking the time to plumb.

When we returned to Nathalie's room I went right up to the bedside and took hold of her hand. She had long fingers and beautiful fingernails. Her hands were cool and she looked more rested and comfortable than she had been. She wasn't on any blood products but was still receiving saline. Her shunt (she'd had one put into the left side of her chest) was being tested/flushed. She was on pain medication every four hours. However, after three hours her right kidney gave her a lot of pain so that she wanted to be massaged for relief.

Are doctors still afraid of medicating people with a terminal illness with sufficient drugs to keep them pain free for fear they'll become addicted? Even after studies show this simply doesn't happen? If by some miracle the person does recover they are not addicted to whatever drug they've been given during their illness. It makes me so angry to think this young woman suffers needless pain because of the possible Philistine, ignorant or insipid attitudes of otherwise intelligent doctors. According to Elisabeth Kubler-Ross, the noted American psychiatrist who brought the word 'death' out of the closet [and author of a number of books including Death: The Final Stage of Growth (Prentice Hall, Englewood Cliffs, NJ, 1975),] a wise doctor seeks to find a level of pain medication which will render the patient pain free without, if at all possible, losing consciousness or being 'out of it'. Naturally this implies several things, including that the doctor cares enough to do this and takes the necessary time and effort to arrive at the correct dosage. More, it suggests they will take the time to monitor the dosage as the pain increases with the disease's progression and change it accordingly. Finally, it suggests the doctor has some skill at symptom and pain control. Many doctors don't.

It's been said that doctors and others in the helping professions become doctors because of their own fear of death and rather than confronting it and dealing with its reality they continue to deny it. These doctors are unable to move from actively working to cure the patient to a place of providing palliative care. It seems to me that not only does the patient suffer but so does the doctor.

Bernie Siegel, M.D. author of 'Love, Medicine and Miracles' (G.K. Hall, Boston, Mass. 1988) talks compassionately about this very subject. Siegel maintains his humanity by acknowledging, honouring and respecting the humanity of his patients.

I told Nathalie how beautiful her brown eyes were and she told me she'd always wanted blue ones. We laughed about not being satisfied with what we've been given. She said she loved Rob's deep blue eyes. Her dark eyes shone as she related to me that Rob was in University and this was 'crunch' time. Although this meant he couldn't come to see her as often as she'd like she said she loved him more 'this way' meaning I think, as a man wanting to 'better himself'.

Every now and then she would take my hand in both of hers and gently stroke it. I was laughing – quietly as she didn't like loud noises. She told me that on Saturday morning a nurse had come bounding into her room at 7 a.m. Nathalie was in a deep sleep. This nurse put on the bright overhead light and sang out in a loud voice,

'GOOD MORNING. TIME FOR BREAKFAST. ' Since Nathalie isn't eating anything except cold cucumbers and drinking fluids this seemed a thoughtless thing to do. I told Nathalie that many people, even nurses and doctors, are uncomfortable when someone is very ill. They stay away or when they come to visit they don't know what to say. I told her that I was this way. However, I assured her that if she could arrange to get well physically and then 'go crazy' I'd be right by her side. She murmured, "I'll see what I can do."

"I want to have visitors, Aunt Joan," she said, "but I don't want them to stay very long or be loud."

I said after about ten minutes, "Well, what do you think; is that enough?"

She smiled her sweetest smile and said she thought it was.

Guy and I left the hospital and drove to Amherstburg to a craft party where the wife of a man from Guy's work was selling her painted china. I purchased a tiny plate covered with lavender pansies, and a little grey bear with a lace collar and pearls around her neck. I'll bring it to Nathalie when we visit her again.

I wonder what Nathalie will think when Claude shows up this Thursday with Pierrette? I'm also expecting Germaine's two other sisters, Micheline and Nicole, to begin arriving soon. I know Germaine will be grateful for their help. I wish there was more I could do and I pray each day that God will use me as He sees fit.

November 9, 1999

Guy and I went to the hospital last night from 6 to 8 p.m. to give Gerry a break. Guy stayed in the room with a sleeping Nathalie. I went into the Atrium and worked for an hour on my Horticulture II course toward my master gardener's certificate.

At seven o'clock I went into the room and put on the earphones so I could watch television. I watched some of Royal Canadian Air Farce and ER. Nathalie had to go to the washroom while we were there. Guy helped her and then he rubbed her back for about five minutes or so. Nathalie told Guy he was an angel.

Nathalie is very fatigued and weak. As it gets closer to the four hours between pain pills she becomes increasingly uncomfortable. Perhaps it's just that she needs to go to the washroom? Perhaps we need to be grateful she can go to the toilet. At least that shows her kidneys are still functioning.

Germaine told me over the phone yesterday that she's going to speak to the doctor because she doesn't think Nathalie is getting any better. Upon reflection, I found this a curious thing to say since Nathalie has just begun chemotherapy. She does seem better to me. But then everything's relative— somewhat better than she's been which hasn't been too well at all.

Germaine arrived at the hospital at 7:45 p.m. looking rested. She and Guy went out to the waiting room for about half an hour.

Nathalie doesn't like the light on or loud noises so we've tried to keep the light off as much as possible. When the chemo had finished two nurses came in to remove the bags from the IV stand. I saw that the nurse removing the brown bag containing the drugs had on thick latex gloves. She slipped off these gloves and together with the chemo bag put them into a box on the room's wall. I thought, the nurse wouldn't even touch the apparatus but poor Nathalie now has that poison in her body. It was expected to help her as it did during two remissions of this devastating disease.

Wasn't it supposed to help her?

> *A simple child,*
> *That lightly draws its breath,*
> *And feels its life in every limb,*
> *What should it know of death?*

William Wordsworth (as quoted in John Walsh's book 'Tears of Rage' 1997 Pocket Books, a division of Simon and Schuster, Inc.)

November 10, 1999

Nathalie will not be going home. It's important 'to be strong' for Nathalie, Germaine said. Is this newest bit of advice straight from the doctors? Now they're saying Nathalie doesn't know how little time she has.

Assholes. WE know THAT. We can't talk about it. We can't cry. We can't express our true thoughts or feelings except to each other. I get so angry. This unwillingness or inability to tell the truth gets in the way of real communion with Nathalie.

We've discovered that going to the hospital around dinnertime, 6 p.m. to be precise, is a good time to find free parking on the street instead of the ridiculous price charged for parking in the lot(s).

Gerry went to the bank today to see about Nathalie's bank account and what can be done about it. She doesn't have a will and they don't want to bring this up with her unless it's absolutely necessary. Given the existing 'rule' that we must not cry or talk about dying, I'm not sure when that would be. Gerry also spoke about going to the funeral home to make arrangements for Nathalie's funeral. I felt sick when I heard him say this. It felt as if time has suddenly warped.

I wondered if Nathalie had been an old woman if the talk about prearranging the funeral would have upset me so much. It wouldn't have bothered me if Nathalie had been the one to ask her parents to take care of the funeral arrangements prior to her death. If there were open discussion about Nathalie's impending death she would have the opportunity to say what she'd like to happen. She'd have a hand in the preparations. There's something about doing this task while she's still alive which feels obscene.

I offered to go with Gerry when he said he would be going alone. No matter my feelings no one should have to go through this alone. I knew instinctively that he wouldn't take me up on my offer but I still felt led to do so, telling him when I'd be available.

Turns out it was the doctor who advised them to make the funeral arrangements now 'while they have the strength'! I can't believe the arrogance of some doctors! It leaves me speechless. I learned when I was a therapist that advice-giving is something to be avoided at all costs. But when I felt I had no choice I would warn my client as to what I was doing! Warned them to take my advice at their own peril – AND mine.

In spite of the medication not meeting her pain level,

Nathalie refused to allow the doctors to put her on a morphine drip. I wonder how long she'll go before she relents? It's becoming increasingly difficult for the nurses to find a vein to give Nathalie what's required 'to keep her alive'. They spent nearly an hour trying to insert the needle. Nathalie is terrified of the pain.

I still struggle with keeping my feelings in check as Nathalie's requested. What's the purpose of this? It feels dishonest to me and may be one of the reasons I have so much trouble entering her room – spending time with her. If I felt I could let my tears fall I might be able to spend time with her. What's wrong with us that we're so ashamed of our feelings, especially our tender ones? It seems endemic to Western 'civilization' that we don't give expression to our feelings in a way appropriate to the given situation. We pretend that we're 'fine thanks'. We're congratulated for 'being strong' as if to be sad and let people know is 'weak'.

No wonder people jump off buildings, blow their brains out, kill their schoolmates or the guy in the next car who just cut them off. There is no safe place for the expression of feelings without resorting to violence.

When will we ever learn?

I remember something Elisabeth Kubler-Ross said in the "Life, Death, Transition" workshop in Winnipeg in 1984. She said that there should be a room in every hospital, prison, old age home, residential treatment centre, Hospice, even our homes where a person can go to express their rage and pained hatred. The room would be called 'The Screaming Room'. It would be padded and filled with thick telephone books and a length of rubber hose. The person would be shown how to use the hose on the books by placing the image of the thing/person they are enraged with and carefully bringing down the hose on the telephone books screaming out their anguish as they do so. As the negative energy is unblocked and courses through their body, it is replaced with a sense of calm serenity which is spiritual in nature. They come to see we have been created with both positive and negative energy. When we do this kind, or any kind, of energy work we are transforming, literally, our negative energy into positive energy.

Gerry, Guy and I spent time in the Atrium.

The Atrium is a room created for 4 North Palliative Care patients, their families and friends though it is visited by people from all over the hospital. It is an oasis in the desert of the dying. A 25' *Ficus Benjamina* 'Weeping Fig' which seems to climb out of the floor reaches for the sun under just one of several skylights. The whisper of running water brings its coolness to a wounded spirit. The room divides into several and is filled with plants of every description. Corn plant, *Dracena marginata*, Croton, Kentea palm, Peace lily, Elephant palm, even Mother's-in-law tongue surround the Rattan couches, chairs, tables and ottomans. An aquarium with tiny coloured fish is its focal point.

The Atrium leads outside to several outdoor patios. Wooden planter boxes overflow with flowers and plants in the growing season. Chairs, tables and benches also made of wood provide a place to sit in conversation, enjoy a moment's solitude with one's lunch and a drink, bask in the hot Windsor sun, enjoy the coolness of spring or autumn's wistfulness.

During the day the atmosphere is one of hope. People laugh frequently. Children may play with the puzzles. Adults may close their eyes or read a book.

In the evening the Atrium takes on an air of mystery as day turns into night; light melts into darkness. There is a sense of peace – an acceptance of life's inevitable ending being lived just a breath away. Though sorrow is close to the surface of the skin, perhaps closer, there is a sense of the 'rightness' of the seasons of life.

I have come to believe that timing is everything.

As Gerry and Guy worked on a puzzle with Gerry chatting away in French, I worked on my final assignment for Horticulture II. After a time, Germaine came in and said she'd be spending the night with Nathalie. Nathalie doesn't want visitors anymore except the odd friend, Rob and her immediate family. Understanding this, I began to pack up to go home just as Gerry said he was going home to get some sleep. The problem was that once Gerry realized we were leaving, too, he decided to stay. Once again I'd acted impulsively. I wished I'd waited.

I've come to the place where all I want is to be in the Atrium working on my courses for the master gardener's certificate. I'm at peace with not being with Nathalie since I feel confident she's already said goodbye to me. She is now slowly withdrawing from family and friends until her final moment. This withdrawing is common with people who are dying. It is a letting go of everything and everyone to whom we've become attached in this physical reality. Jeannie says dying is like 'folding your tent'.

This morning Guy and I had an emotional time over breakfast. Or perhaps said more correctly, I cried and carried on while Guy remained stoic. I'm the overly emotional half of this relationship and know I wouldn't be if Guy would own his own feelings and express them. Time with my therapist has shown me that when one person in a relationship refuses to have certain feelings the other has to carry the entire load him or her self. It's a burden to carry my own emotions, never mind carrying his too.

I'm also becoming aware that a lot of the emotion I'm feeling right now isn't associated with Nathalie at all. It's about my daughter and her rejection of me. The strong emotional charge comes because we're estranged and I could die before there is any healing of this chasm. More than that, what if she dies before me? How would I ever cope? I don't think I would and I'm powerless to change her. I've tried everything I can think of short of driving to her home and slapping her upside the head. Something I'm ashamed to say I'd done more than once in her teen years. She joked with me later in life that I had a wicked backhand. It was no joke. What I did was abusive.

Guy called some of his siblings last night. I was stunned with the matter-of-fact manner with which he conveyed the news about Nathalie. Since they aren't aware of how ill she is his call had to be a shock. Micheline, his next youngest sister, was crying when he said goodbye.

I'm struggling, too, with my feelings about his sisters. On the one hand I'm pissed off that they aren't more supportive in a practical way to Germaine. On the other hand I'd like them to stay away forever. The growing intimacy between Germaine, Gerry, Guy and I is so lovely I don't want it broken by other family members. I'm so hungry for closeness that like a greedy child I don't think it can expand but that it retracts when others enter the picture. Yet I want his sisters to take turns coming to Germaine's house and taking care of things for her. Cleaning, cooking, shopping, walking the dog, whatever is required to lighten her burden. This is what I would do if I were her sister. If my sister, Jeannie, needed me I'd do what Mama did when Guy was in hospital. I'd just be there for her. No questions. But I'm NOT her sister and never will be.

"When you do this unto the least of these my brethren you do it unto me."   Matthew 25:40.

Because of my conviction that a person who is dying should be told the truth Guy's frightened I might blurt it out to Nathalie. This hurts me very much as I'd hoped he knew me better. But then perhaps he does and that's reason enough to be worried!

November 11, 1999
The vigil continues.

Tonight as I studied in the Atrium a family was gathered in the circle of chairs next to my table. One of its elder members was the patient. But it was the little boy who caught my attention. He was about 3 years old and blond. He was sitting on the floor in the centre of the circle. The four adults surrounding him appeared to be his mother, father, grandfather and grandmother.

This little fellow was an absolute delight. I'd just finished eating a MacDonald's Happy Meal. They come with a small toy. I offered the toy to him. He smiled and said, 'Thank you' in English spiced with a Hungarian accent.

This child's presence brought a breath of life to a place

where death dwells. His sun-kissed hair and sweet smile were a balm to my wounded heart, a moment's forgetfulness.

I can see him, his innocence intact, untouched by life's realities. He carried no visible fear. His joy was contagious making me laugh with childlike exuberance. He had been cushioned in love.

Life is paradox. Joy holds hands with suffering in a chair of comfort and pain. It's true that I wouldn't recognize the child's joy if I hadn't also experienced suffering.

I remember pictures of myself when Guy was ill and we were filled with sorrow that he wouldn't live more than a year; I was more beautiful than I'd been since I was a young woman of 19. I didn't understand this mystery then and don't now.

Nathalie was much improved yesterday, even eating a little just to please her parents who keep racking their brains trying to tempt her with food they hope she'll eat. She really wants nothing except fluids. Before leaving the hospital I went into her room to say goodnight. My presence startled her so that I realized she hadn't known I was in the Atrium doing what I'm meant to do.

Tonight, Germaine talked at length about the hope that a miracle would be granted and Nathalie would come home strong and healthy once more. This hope remains in spite of the doctor quite purposefully taking Germaine aside and reiterating that Nathalie will not be leaving the hospital. The word 'alive' hangs like a spider web one pretends one can't see. She mustn't get her hopes up. Germaine looked at me with questioning in her eyes clearly wanting me not to leave her in despair. Not really knowing what to say, I said that doctors don't know everything. Miracles do happen – look at Guy. She smiled, 'That's right!'

At least do not harm!

The wise words of a beloved Social Work professor and Psychotherapist, echo in my head. I don't know when/if Nathalie is going to die. My role here is to be supportive and loving. A constant presence at a time when listening is in short supply. Isn't it always? Most of us are too busy and self-centered to waste a moment being open to another's cares. I'm here with a mother whose 'baby girl' is dying.

People will have to begin doing the calling to Windsor because Germaine has gotten tough. She doesn't have the time or energy to keep them updated about Nathalie's condition. I feel blessed that Guy and I have been given the opportunity to walk this journey with Germaine and Nathalie. It feels like a gift from God. I wonder if this sounds funny to people who haven't – yet – been through a similar experience? I wonder at some people's unwillingness to do the same? Jeannie says that we make a decision over and over whether to truly 'live' or just to stay at our established comfort level. She learned this as a Palliative Care volunteer walking with a man dying of AIDS over a period of eighteen months. This man I'll call Joe* was an active alcoholic. He was often nasty and rude. Sometimes Jeannie cried with me over the telephone before visiting him in hospital. He died nearly five years ago. Jeannie 'wouldn't have missed it for the world'. Joe died holding her hand, completely at peace. He had grown to accept that Jeannie's love was genuine. An open love which asked nothing in return. This was so foreign to Joe it took a long time for him to accept. It also took many testings of Jeannie to convince him of the love's authenticity.

Claude and Pierrette are arriving today and Germaine said Pierrette will be doing some cooking for them.

I sometimes find myself angry that children don't help their parents more – especially grown children. Then I see Martin 'Marty', Nathalie's only brother. Her big brother. He's going to the hospital from 11 a.m. to 2:30 p.m. when he has to leave to go to work. Nathalie has been telling her parents what a special time this is with Marty and how she appreciates how hard he tries. And he does. Marty's metamorphosis is happening right before our eyes. He is rising to another level of spiritual growth. Marty's like a shining star becoming brighter and brighter every day. It's wonderful to be an eyewitness to the change.

Gerry has met with the bank manager who has assured

him that when the time comes there will be no problems with accessing Nathalie's bank account. There is no life insurance for the coming expenses so the few thousand dollars will help to allay the cost of a funeral, cemetery plot and marker. Something none of us wants even to think about.

I had lunch with my friend, Kate*, today. She pointed out to me the importance of being present at these times in a person's lifetime. We are being honoured when we're invited to be a part of their dying. There is so much spiritual growth to be gained from the experience in spite of the sharp pain and sorrow one feels. Kate nursed both her mother and grandmother in their final illnesses.

I know from going through Guy's cancer – renal cell carcinoma – and the removal of his left kidney in '83 as well as Mom and Dad's deaths that there is also great joy mingled with sadness at these times in one's life. It is an intensely painful and beautiful time juxtaposed with the routine of everyday life. It parallels the Easter and Christmas services at church. The days of Ordinary time are wedged between special liturgies for Holy Thursday, Good Friday and the Easter Vigil. Sacred rituals, beautifully coloured vestments, living plants including fragrant Easter lilies and Christmas trees lit with hundreds of lights. The altar is draped with cloths representing the specific time in the church's calendar, purple for Lent, white for Easter and Christmas. Each of these times so much a part of a person's life fabric neither to be avoided or shunned but to be entered into fully and deeply even when one is afraid. Especially when one is afraid? To stay in one's comfort zone and to avoid stepping out into the unknown restricts and limits one's life. Is it that person who on their deathbed realizes with chilling regret that they are dying without having lived?

Though I feel in my bones that Nathalie said goodbye to me last Sunday, even I wonder when she seems so much better today.

For the first time Gerry told me that he feels Germaine is looking better and how much he believes it's because she has needed to talk with me. Both Germaine and Gerry have said they don't know how they'll react once Nathalie is dead. I've assured them that no matter how they behave it will be okay. I've said Guy and I will be there for them when they need us. The birth of Chantal's baby will be wonderful and I know they will spend more time with her and their first grandchild. I feel it will be such a wonderful blessing.

'The Lord giveth and the Lord taketh away. Blessed be the name of the Lord'

What is it about these words from the Book of Job that keep repeating in my ears?

I got an ego boost when Gerry said he didn't know I was taking the courses to become a master gardener. He seemed impressed and to take pleasure in what I was doing.

November 12, 1999

Guy dropped me off at the hospital on his way to the Ciociaro Club for the 2nd United Way get-together of this season's fundraiser. Rob was sitting in Nathalie's darkened room reading a book in the window's light. Rob's a quiet, shy young man. Blond to Nathalie's brunette.

When I entered the Atrium I realized why it was empty. It was freezing. The drop in temperatures yesterday was reflected in this usually comfortable room. I checked the fish to be sure they were still swimming silently in the unlit aquarium. Do fish need the dark at night the same as we do?

Pierrette came into the Atrium, having arrived in Windsor with Claude about 2:30 p.m. She looked good to me at that moment though later at Germaine's house she look sad and tired.

"How do you find Nathalie?" I asked, curious to know how someone who isn't with her nearly every day would find her. Pierrette, Nathalie's aunt, said she found her very thin.

I find my dear French-Canadian family masters of understatement.

Recently Pierrette became involved with a volunteer group to raise funds for unrelated bone marrow and organ transplant donors. Guy sponsored her in one event—a Dragon Boat Race.

In a positive and productive way, Pierrette took her sorrow and channeled it into a potentially life-saving project. It might not save her niece but she grabbed hold of the opportunity to use her grief to help others.

She is a hero to me.

It is too easy to blame, to find fault and lament one's lot in life in order to deflect one's pain on to another.

When Claude, Guy's eldest brother, arrived he looked fit and strong, the result of mushing with his twelve Huskies at his home in Northern Ontario. Evidence of the leukemia he suffers doesn't show and like the rest of the men in this family he makes light of it when we bring it up in conversation.

He had to go back to his truck for the sign and mailbox Nelly painted for Guy and I. On the underside of the sign were the words, "Happy 25th Anniversary, Guy and Joan". Both gifts are really beautiful, covered with pansies, one of my favourite flowers. Their faces perpetually upturned to the sun. The sign and mailbox are too beautiful to put out in Windsor's hot summer and cold winter weather.

Germaine arrived looking tired, dark circles under her eyes. It was clear yesterday's hope had melted away as Nathalie had had a very difficult night. She needed morphine put into her oxygen mask. Twice.

She still won't take the morphine drip.

I moved to the warmer lending library and was reading a book about the trees in Windsor and Essex County when Guy arrived earlier than anticipated. For the first time since Nathalie's battle I felt restless and wanted to leave the hospital. We decided to visit Germaine, Claude and Pierrette at Germaine's house. We needed to be out of the largely sterile atmosphere into the warmth of a home with our family.

Pierrette was cooking a large pot of vegetable soup when we arrived. We sat together around the kitchen table eating the hot satisfying soup with Nelly's homemade bread covered with butter. Absolutely delicious.

For the first time in my presence Germaine began to cry, saying over and over again, "I can't believe it. I can't believe it".

I was going to leave her for a few moments so she could feel the weight of her grief and then I would have put my arms around her really tight. But Pierrette immediately went to her and began stroking her shoulder.

Pierrette is looking for work and said she had an interview on Monday.

Marty came home from work and you can see the changes Nathalie's illness has created in him. They are marked forever in his face. With the rest of the adults talking I said quietly to Marty, 'You're a good boy.'

"Tell my mother," he said.

"You're good to go to be with your sister every day."

"You got to do what you got to do," he said.

Malabouchi is Japanese for 'Just Do It'. This is my daughter-in-law, Debbie's, mantra. She holds a second degree black belt in Aikido.

Poor little Simkin, Germaine's dog, has been left alone so much that seeing everyone tonight has been a tail wagging treat. Finding no food for her, Claude and Guy made ready to drive to the store. Simkin wouldn't leave until Germaine said the magic words in French, "Menez auto, Simkin!" Germaine says Simkin goes downstairs looking for Nathalie in her bedroom and seems puzzled that she can't find her there.

It was comforting to sit with Claude, Pierrette, Guy and Germaine chatting. For a time we could pretend that our hearts weren't breaking or that our lives weren't about to change irrevocably.

I recalled how Nathalie had told me that all she wanted was for her family to be close to each other. To love each other. She found it sad that this was beginning to happen but that she was too ill to enjoy it. She didn't say dying though the word hung in the air like an apple at the end of a fragile branch. She begged me – no I don't think that's too strong a word – to visit with her mom and get her to go out and do things – to enjoy her life – not to waste it. I assured her I'd do my best, but, of course, I couldn't make Germaine do anything she didn't want to do. Nathalie acknowledged the truth of my words with a wistful smile.

A phrase kept running through my head until I wrote it down. I think it might have had something to do with the fact that yesterday was Remembrance Day, and also with the fact that I go to the hospital and sit in the Atrium doing my studies. I did quite a bit of studying yesterday and on the surface, it seemed to be of little help. 'They also serve who only sit and wait.' I believe these words arose from the ashes of the Second World War referring to the families who stayed home waiting for their men to return. I just know, for myself, that I'm doing what I feel led to do one day at a time.

Perhaps I'll ask to sit with Nathalie before too long?

Last night Germaine was fretting. She wondered whether she'd deprived Nathalie of the chance to say or do what she needed to do before she dies. I told Germaine about Elisabeth Kubler-Ross' suggestion to ask the question, "Would you like to talk about it?" Worded as a question it leaves the person the freedom to respond in whatever way suits them. Germaine doesn't want to do anything that would hurt Nathalie in any way.

I don't know if she ever asked.

Nat wants Rob in her room but she doesn't want to talk to him. She's not talking very much right now because when she does she starts to cough. It's clearly painful for her.

Was it my imagination or did Germaine talk more to me than to her sister? The brothers and sisters all spoke together several times in French but Germaine also spoke often to me in English. She told me about the cross stitch Nathalie had done for her cousin's wedding gift when she marries in July next year. Germaine said the piece was finished except for the wedding rings. It will need to be framed, too. This gift will be very precious and an heirloom over time from a beautiful, artistic, sweet young woman. A young woman who will never marry or have children. A woman expressing her love for her cousin and future husband. Nathalie was creating memories to last forever.

Whatever made me think she didn't know she was dying?

November 13, 1999

Guy and I went to the hospital at 5:20 p.m. yesterday staying until ten minutes to seven. The Atrium was cold and the lending library locked so we went into Nathalie's room. An exhausted Germaine went home to try and rest. The television was on and Nat was picking at her food, waiting for some Gravol that the nurse had to put into the IV. I watched as a nursing student mixed the medicine under the RN's supervision long after Nathalie had eaten half her soup, drank her milk and eaten a few tortellini.

More talkative than she's been with me for some time, Nathalie said she sometimes watches TV to help her with 'the rough spots'. I asked her what she meant. She didn't say. I wondered for the hundredth time if she really was hungry and wanted to eat or if she was eating because she thought she should or because her parents encourage her? As we watched The Drew Carey Show we made the occasional burst of small talk. Then Nathalie began to wonder aloud when she would be going home. She said she usually went home after the chemotherapy was finished but this time the doctor wasn't saying she could go home yet. This didn't fit the usual pattern and rhythm of her life for the past two years. She was puzzled. I asked her if she wanted to go home. She said she did. However, there was a proviso. In the hospital she has the security of knowing that emergency help is immediately available. The pull of home with its comfort and familiarity and the need for safety and security created ambiguity within her.

I'm thinking, does she need to know she's dying and not going home? Does going home mean her earthly or heavenly home? Is she speaking symbolically? Have people with her cancer and at its apparently advanced stage gone home? How long do they expect her to live? These are questions I'd like someone to attempt to answer even if they're wrong, and even if they don't know for sure! After all, Nathalie though young isn't a child and I believe she has a right to know whatever is known about her condition. It's as if here I, too, have forgotten the doctor telling Germaine that they would try to keep Nathalie alive until Christmas!

As we were talking at a deeper level than we had up until now, Gerry walked in. His arrival was unexpected. Our conversation was over. Would it ever begin again? I wasn't to know I'd been granted a greater gift. The rare privilege of being with a young woman and her father talking openly and honestly with each other in my presence. Nathalie spoke with such immediacy and intimacy about a variety of topics. Gerry's family was not known by Nathalie very well. Gerry spoke about his brother's apparent lack of interest in spending time with him when Gerry took the time to travel each summer to Quebec.

This hurt Gerry a lot.

Nathalie spoke about how Chantal, Martin and she didn't really get along very well with their father and how since she'd been sick she'd grown closer to him and how nice that was for her. For Gerry too. When he'd come into the room he'd said he came back to the hospital because he missed his daughter. These were his exact words.

Nathalie has grown closer to Marty, too. She said she sometimes thought he was a bit of a drip but that we all could be from time to time and that Marty had actually come to the place where he kissed her goodbye when he left the hospital to go to work. She said that what is happening now with her family is what she always wanted to happen. She's very glad they are becoming closer to each other.

Me too.

I could see that Nathalie was beginning to close her eyes so I suggested it was time to leave. Nathalie called me over close to her bed.

"I'm glad, Aunt Joan, that you came back," referring to the many years I'd had little contact with my in-laws and their families.

I told her, "So am I."

In reading my meditation book by Sheldon Kopp, "Blues Ain't Nothing But a Good Soul Feeling Bad."(1992, Fireside

Books) and his quote, "All we know is what we imagine to be true." I thought about Nathalie. We imagine that Nathalie is dying and will not be with us for very much longer. How much longer? We don't know. Nathalie isn't saying she's dying. At least she's not saying these actual words. Who knows what's really goes on inside of her. Death is not on the minds of most young people. Does this include young people who are dying? They think they're indestructible or as I once heard Margaret Atwood say on television, that they'll die before they're 30 in a 'blaze of glory'!

I find myself – to my everlasting shame – wanting her to go into a coma so I can sit quietly with her and hold her hand. Somehow I'd feel safer if she were sicker and I didn't have to hold back my feelings pretending I'm not heart broken. I wish I didn't mind sitting with her now while she can still talk with me but all my life I've abhorred physical illness of any kind. I want to run when I'm in its presence.

I've decided I won't go to the hospital this weekend. Germaine will have lots of family support with Chantal, Darrin, Remy and Nicole arriving from out-of-town. Next week Germaine will once again need Guy and I when everyone else has returned to their own lives and routines.

November 14, 1999
We had dinner at Sir Cedric's yesterday after 5:30 p.m. mass. Guy called Germaine and we went to visit with her and Nicole. Chantal and Darrin were at the hospital with Nathalie. Germaine likes having family with Nathalie so she's not alone. I wonder if Nat ever wants to be alone?

We played a game of Joker Rummy and this lifted Germaine's tired spirits. She couldn't play real poker because she gets so excited when she has a good hand! Germaine makes me laugh a lot whenever we play cards together. She's a damn good card player! Most of the members are in this family. The game was often interrupted by the insistent ringing of the telephone. An aunt calling from Quebec. A sister-in-law from Montreal. Finally, Darrin's Mom. Germaine can tell when the call is long distance because of a difference in the rings. I don't hear it.

Nicole said she hoped she'd never have to go through what Germaine's going through. I agreed. No one would wish this pain on anyone.

Gerry, Marty, Remy and sometimes Guy were playing a game on the computer called Roller Coaster. Guy seemed quite taken with it. Gerry eventually went downstairs to watch television. Television seems to be a way for him to be alone and quiet. A way to distance himself from the present reality of his life. A way to recoup his inner resources so that he can go on.

Germaine wasn't sure if she was going to spend the night at the hospital. Apparently earlier on Nat had said her mom wouldn't have to come back since she was feeling pretty good. Germaine said she sleeps better at the hospital where she's close to Nathalie and the nurses. Germaine was restless waiting to hear from Chantal as to whether or not Nat wanted her back. We suggested she might get some rest at home.

What do we know?

Nathalie is getting morphine in her oxygen. Marty said she was in pain when he was there.

Standing in the foyer of Germaine's home saying goodbye – a lovely family tradition – Marty said that tomorrow we'd be back to the old routine. Everyone would be going back home today. I wonder if Marty's sad about this return? Unashamedly I realize I'm not. I like the time alone with Germaine, Gerry, Marty, Guy and I. I've come to enjoy the intimacy we've created caring each in our own way for Nathalie and in so doing caring for each other as well.

Next week I'm busy every night. I don't know what I'm going to do about visiting the hospital. I'm not available when I'm needed which is right after Marty leaves to go to work until Gerry arrives from work. Much as I wish I were able to be there, there's a part of me that's glad for the break.

November 15, 1999

Guy and I went to the hospital last night around 6 staying with Nathalie until 8:10 p.m. When we arrived Chantal was there. Nat was sitting on the side of the bed looking frail and forlorn like a flower in need of a refreshing rain. She said she was going to walk around in the corridors of the hospital. I was really surprised since she doesn't even go to the toilet in her room. She uses a commode which is just a few feet from her bed. Her feet were swollen with edema. What causes this to happen? She wasn't wearing the oxygen mask nor did she have any needles in her body except for the one for the saline. Is this just to keep her hydrated? She'd had two nosebleeds and had vomited once during the day. She needed platelets. For the first time in a while she'd spent the night alone so Germaine could stay at home. Nathalie said she knew how much her mom needed a break.

I couldn't help wondering if Nathalie is venturing outside her room and eating a little more because she wants to go home so much or to please her parents or because she's feeling better?

Chantal is beginning to look pregnant. Her baby is due in April. She showed us an ultrasound picture of her baby, looking for all the world like a little alien with huge eye sockets. It is amazing what can be done today with modern technology.

Initially I went to the Atrium and it wasn't as cold as it has been the past few nights. The lending library was closed. I worked for a while on the question in my final assignment for Hort II on native trees, shrubs and plants. I'm definitely going to have to do more research on this question as the book is just trees and a few shrubs. After about 45 minutes Guy came and asked me to come visit Nat, as he felt he was too boring for her. Chantal was gone. Their car has been presenting problems and once her husband, Darrin, got the car started he didn't want to take a chance and shut it off. They had a three hour trip in front of them.

Nathalie had said she enjoys having deep philosophical talks. She even referred to our talk a few nights earlier. It turns out Nathalie is very frustrated. She wants to go home. One of the doctors she sees every morning has been quite blunt with her but either without enough clarity as to Nathalie's true condition or Nat doesn't want to hear what the doctor has to say.

Nathalie talked about going home and beginning to decorate the house and tree slowly so she could relish every moment. And because she doesn't have the strength to do it any other way? She spoke about loving Christmas. What it meant to her. Family, love, giving, tradition were just a few things. Gift-giving was delightful when she was a child but it was no longer the most important thing. Not for the first time she said she felt her sickness had brought her family closer together. She acknowledged that though it wasn't the ideal way to bring a family together, she was grateful for it just the same. She hoped it wouldn't go away when she got better.

I said that often when someone needs us very much like when we're ill then we, the family, will rally round that person in order to be of whatever help we can. But once the crisis is over we return to our own lives with our routines and personal interests. I said this seemed to be the way we were. The intensity of involvement during times like these could not be lived out by us for too long or we would become too tired to function, inviting illness for ourselves, too.

Nathalie said that she had long distance friends whom she hadn't called to let know that she was ill once again. She said she really didn't feel like telephoning them. If they wanted to talk to her they'd have to do the calling. She spoke about Chantal's baby, her niece or nephew, and how much she's looking forward to seeing 'it'.

All the time she was talking in a way that set her apart from everything surrounding her, as if she was in the centre of a cloud unseen by the eye. She seemed to wear her sadness like a cloak. What I would clinically call denial on her part was tinged with pathos. It left me wondering if she really believed she was going to get well but rather that she knew she would not be going home. Or even if by some miracle she did go home she would not live too much longer.

I wonder when the word 'home' is used in relation to Nathalie or by Nathalie herself if home is not the home she's known all these years but quite another place not of this world. The place she was before she was born and the place she'll return to when she dies.

Now the least effort exhausts her. One of the reasons she stopped walking to the bathroom next to her room. She has to have two x-rays today of her lungs and abdomen. The effort required will tax her waning strength.

The doctors are concerned about her bowel movements. They are liquid. I wonder what they expect when she barely eats? They are concerned she might have a bowel impaction and so want to see just what's happening.

I wonder if it's not important to tell her what they believe is going to happen even if it doesn't?

Last night I often felt like a fraud knowing what I know and not being able to speak with Nathalie from a deeply honest place. I'm afraid when she discovers how ill she really is and that she isn't expected to get better or even leave the hospital that she'll be very angry with us for holding back this information. What does being so careful with Nathalie do to Germaine's energy? I know that a person holding on to energy needing expression pays a price in their body. The body suffers physically, emotionally and spiritually. I learned this myself in the years I did bioenergetic work. Let's hope that today or tomorrow something is said so that we can all be honest with her and give her the opportunity to finish whatever it is that needs finishing.

I just called my sister, Jeannie, and told her how sad I was. She said that Nathalie is just where she needs to be right now. I wish I could remember that it isn't my place to DO anything except offer my love and support where I can and wherever it's needed.

I wonder if I'll ever forget Nathalie's sweet, sad, smiling face as she struggles to make sense of what's happening to her? Of her deep desire to love? To live her own life independent of her family? Of wanting to make her own way in the world and

to leave her mark? All of which are being denied her. I'm
amazed that I don't cry out my own grief. Yet in spite of
feeling a few times that I would, I didn't.

November 16, 1999

Guy went to the hospital last night from 7 to 9 p.m., spending
an hour in the Atrium with Germaine while Rob was with
Nathalie. I was at the St. Leonard's House Board of Directors'
meeting.

Nathalie will be going home at the end of the week with
oxygen and IV. A nurse who has cared for her in the past will
be coming to care for her. Nathalie wants to stay in her own
bed. The hospital has made it clear she can have a hospital bed.
I expect it will come to that if (a) she's able to go home at the
end of the week, or (b) she doesn't have to go back to the
hospital. She is scheduled for more chemotherapy on December
6th. She seems improved.

Apparently the doctors told Germaine that if Nat's 'big' on
going home she'll be sent home as a last wish. Does this
contradict what I've just written? The prevailing theme seems
to be that she's not going to survive for too much longer.
Germaine both anticipates and is nervous about having
Nathalie at home. I would be terrified if I were in her place.

There are no results from the x-rays.

I wonder if the doctor believes Nathalie will go home at all
or if she's saying this simply to quiet Nathalie?

I can feel the wisdom of not going to the hospital for a
while. It gives Guy a chance to spend time with Germaine.
Tonight he's babysitting our grandsons, Matthew and Brandon.
He could still go to the hospital after our son, Blake, gets home.

I'm feeling really tired and wish I didn't have quite so
much to do this week. I don't like going out every night. It
feels like too much for me. I'm glad I have the day at home
tomorrow in order to finish the article on Art Roth's creation of
the garden at St. Clare R. C. School, both for my writing class
and for the master gardeners' column.

November 18, 1999

Today is Guy's birthday. He's 53. He went to the hospital last night around 7 and stayed until just after 9. Germaine became ill the night before and was at home unable to come to the hospital. I do wish they'd get some help from the Hospice. Micheline, Guy's younger sister, is coming today but we don't know how long she's planning to stay. I hope it's for a few days perhaps even over the entire weekend. I'll be going up again on Friday. I haven't been to the hospital since Sunday night. I've enjoyed the time away. I feel it's important for me to take a break from everyone and everything. I'll be ready to go back on Friday.

Nathalie wasn't very talkative last night. Guy sat and read while she slept on and off. Gerry was there when Guy arrived. Gerry is like a sweet old 'mother' hen bird fussing over 'her' chickadee! I find it quite appealing. Nathalie had to wait all day yesterday and the day before for platelets. Lack of availability, I think. Guy and I wondered aloud whether she really will be going home. I believe it might be too much for Germaine with the additional concern that they aren't immediately accessible to medical aid.

I do wish they'd tell Nathalie the truth. Whatever they deem it to be. I believe this is what's sapping Germaine's energy making it nearly impossible a task to be present to her daughter while keeping this secret in her heart. Wouldn't the truth set them both free? They'd be able to do whatever needs to be done before Nathalie dies.

Is there anything else I should be doing to help? I ask myself this all the time and so far I've not felt I should go to the house unless Nathalie comes home and then I would offer to be there if needed.

If I ever again must go through a similar experience I will come right out and ask questions, like, "Would you like me to clean your house; do your laundry; buy your groceries; walk the dog?" Whatever! It would have been such a simple thing to do.

November 19, 1999

Guy went up to see Nathalie again last night and Rob arrived around 8. I must try to speak to Rob when this is all over. I'd like to know about his relationship with Nathalie. What their relationship meant to him. What he learned from her. How his life has changed because he loved her.

Micheline has arrived. Guy and I will go to the hospital tonight in our usual way – me in the Atrium, Guy in Nathalie's room. Oh I'll go and speak with Nathalie briefly but I don't plan to stay in the room especially if there are others there. Too crowded.

Nathalie told Guy last night that if she were 60 she would let go but because she's just 24 she feels she has to fight. I must try to ask her what she means by 'let go'. Yet isn't this self-evident? I wonder who's in denial now?

Nathalie was getting platelets when Guy arrived but on the whole she seemed about the same - no better, no worse. Her x-rays show that there is no cancer in the abdomen. Not yet, I feel myself add silently. Her lungs are 'just the same', whatever that means. No better? No worse? No better or worse than what? Germaine isn't staying overnight but going in the morning. The nurses told her to come anytime during the night if she needs to be with Nathalie.

Nothing to indicate that Nathalie's going home this weekend but it's only Friday and things can and do change quickly.

November 20, 1999

Last night was the most beautiful of nights. It rained. I pictured the angels crying their tears washing the earth with a cleansing balm. I imagine the trees raising their branches to God in a grateful prayer of thanks.

The door to Nathalie's room had a sign, 'No Visitors, Please. Check with Nursing Station'. Our initial response was one of alarm. Gerry calmed us. He explained the note was because Nathalie was feeling overwhelmed by the number of visitors. Immediate family and Rob are the only people Nat wants to see. Not even close friends are being embraced. Gerry fussed in his sweet and caring way.

Today Nathalie had a shower with help from her Mom and the nurses. She also used the washroom next to her room. She still has hair. She has sores in her mouth and throat. Thrush? She gets something liquid for it every four hours. She asked her nurse, a young man familiar to her, if she could have it sooner. Like all nurses he said the dosage was prescribed under a doctor's order.

She wasn't to receive the next dose until 10 p.m.

He said he'd see if he could get it for her at 9!

I thought immediately of the scene in the movie, Terms of Endearment, when Shirley MacLaine's character is at the nurses' station demanding her dying daughter be given her next pain medication. I have never forgotten the urgency and passion in her voice as she advocated on behalf of her dying daughter.

In the artificial light Nathalie looks yellow to me. Is the light playing tricks on me? This isn't the first time she's looked this way. The effects of the chemo? My breath catches and my heart skips a beat whenever I see the nursing staff with their heavy rubber gloves. They wear them for everything they handle around Nathalie. No one can use her washroom, a sign declaring, "For patient use only, please." I used to think this was for the protection of the visitors!

When I said I'd missed her, not having see her since last Sunday, the 13th, she murmured, "Really" and looked puzzled. I needn't be surprised. I'm seldom in her room at all now. Her intimate circle is growing smaller and smaller as she sheds more of this world's encumbrances.

The only meds she's on are antibiotics through an IV. What infection are they endeavouring to heal or ward off?

Platelets are still being given and Nathalie gives herself a shot in the leg to increase the white blood count.

As I reflect on what's happening in her room I realize that anything Nathalie is being given is palliative in an effort to fulfill the doctor's promise to Germaine, "I'll do my best to keep her alive until Christmas". Poor doctor. Hasn't anyone told her that death wins in the end? That all she's doing is holding off the inevitable. I'm stunned at how patronizing I can be. And how blind! Death never wins. Love does.

Nathalie's look tonight can only be described as wistful.

Again I feel frustrated at being unable to speak candidly with Nathalie. I wish I didn't have to use up all my energy holding back so I won't blurt it out in an unthinking moment. Why? Why don't they tell her? Would it be too real for them? Nathalie would only hear what she wanted to hear. She would continue to deny if that's what she needs to do.

Damn it, I'd feel better!

The little grey teddy bear with evening pearls and lace vest lies sleeping in her original wrapping. I've finally let myself know that I'm not going to give her to Nathalie. Not now. Perhaps never.

Guy brought four puzzles to the Atrium. The puzzles already there had missing pieces. There's nothing Guy, the master puzzle solver, hates more.

Later, Gerry, Nat and I were in her room, each in separate chairs at the end of the bed. Nathalie spoke to Gerry in French. He reached out putting his arm around the back of her chair gently rubbing her back. At that moment she lay her head against his chest. She was tired of being in bed but too tired to sit up for long. Gerry helped her back into bed covering her up with the blanket.

Her feet and ankles were badly swollen.

These images never leave me, continuing to haunt, filling me with sadness. I remember again the movie Shadowlands.

Pain is the price one pays later for the joy of loving now.

Although I do try to be reasonable I'm upset that Micheline only stayed overnight returning home yesterday afternoon. I want them to come and help – permanently. A romantic is what Guy calls me. Unrealistic is more blunt! I forget that they have their own lives to live and they mustn't stop doing that. Nathalie has more wisdom than I do about this very thing. I'll bet she'd admonish me and shake her finger at me telling me, "No, no, Aunt Joan, live now."

What did Jesus mean when he said 'Let the dead bury the dead?' I've a tendency to the literal and concrete. I wish I understood the symbolism.

Nathalie was in bed cleaning her teeth while I read my book about trees ripping up little pieces of paper to use as tiny bookmarks. Later I'll compare the trees with the other book. Then I'll choose five trees and shrubs for my final assignment. I want to complete Hort II before the end of the year.

I don't think I'll make it.

The room was quiet. To say I was relaxed and comfortable would be a mistake. I'm far too controlling to be either relaxed or comfortable in a situation where I feel completely out of control. But I was happy to be with Nathalie again. My wish had come true.

Few words were spoken.

I see her still sitting up in bed carefully cleaning each tooth. A mundane ritual elevated to the level of high art. Her long, slender fingers with nails shaped like almonds caressing the tiny brush occasionally spitting into a cup with grace and dignity; no movement wasted. A still life one stands before lost in contemplation. A picture hung forever on the wall of memory.

When Guy returned to the room we watched TV. Friends, The Drew Carey Show and Whose Line Is It Anyway? Nat loves these shows.

I touched Nathalie's foot in farewell. Guy went directly to her, reaching out and gently rubbing the top of her head. Faces inches apart, Guy's bent in admiration, Nathalie reached out to rub his head in return. This parting ritual began last week when Guy visited alone with Nathalie.

November 21, 1999
Exhaustion weighs us down like a dark force.

We went to Germaine's last night and played cards. Gerry was at the hospital. He returned home hungry, needing a shower and pissed off. Our nerves are stressed to the breaking point. Tempers are close to the surface. Guy and Gerry got into a tiff about working on Saturday. Gerry didn't understand how Guy got out of working on Saturdays since the company posted 'full' meaning everyone has to come to work. Guy said he never works on Saturday unless it's what he wants. The truth is he doesn't work Saturday because that's become our day to be together and to do household chores. It's the day we have breakfast at the TBQ, buy our groceries at Zehr's and Remark Farms. It's the day Guy helps me in the garden.

Gerry said Nathalie was doing better. Germaine gave him an odd look. It's clear to us that Germaine doesn't believe Nat's getting better or that she'll be coming home from the hospital. Nathalie did go outside of her room for the first time since entering it several weeks ago. She even sat on a chair for a couple of minutes. Gerry brought their dog, Simkin, to the hospital for half an hour before Nat asked him to take the dog home. The nurses felt Simkin would be a treat for the other patients, too.

I'm feeling that Nat doesn't want any visitors except immediate family and Rob.

Jim's friend in the room next to Nat's 'went sour' on Thursday and had to be taken to intensive care where he's on a respirator. Non-Hodgkins Lymphoma turned to Leukemia and he's unlikely to get better. His blood pressure soared and he either had a virus, bacterial infection or fungal infection. At first they weren't sure which it was. They were eventually able to isolate a fungal infection and it's being treated.

I called Jim from Germaine's and spoke to his wife. She said Jim's very upset with his friend's illness. This kind of situation makes it abundantly clear that none of us has any control over much. Even though we all know we're going to die our egos prevent us truly from taking in the reality of death. Oh sure, it's going to happen SOME day but definitely NOT today.

When I look at Nathalie I see my own death and get scared knowing one day it might be me in a Palliative Care hospital bed. I'm glad I've got the book, "When Things Fall Apart" by Pema Chodron, (Shambhala Publications, Inc.,

Boston, Mass. 1997) a Buddhist nun tells about the Buddhist way of life. It invites me to enter the pain and not resist it. It talks about opening our hearts ever wider, not closing them out of fear of being hurt. Breathing in other people's pain to mingle with our own and breathing out compassion and love for all including ourselves. Meditating and concentrating on the out breath when I feel my anxiety and when thoughts interfere saying simply 'thinking' without judgement or censor.

The sweet smile on Nat's face whenever I see her hides a deep sorrow at the knowledge that her death is near. I don't know if this knowledge is conscious or not but I know it's there. She's not ready to let go.

Not yet.

Germaine said something curious, "It's like it's all beginning again." Later I thought I should have asked if she feared it would never end. In a way I'm glad I didn't think of it at the time. Is she wanting it to end on the one hand, even wishing for it all to end, while on the other hand she hopes it never does?

After Nathalie's cardiac arrest during the time she spent at Princess Margaret Hospital in Toronto I'd asked her what it was like to come face-to-face with death. I wish I had the guts to ask her again! She told me that she'd had an experience where she'd been told she was 'out of it' but she could see her hands and everything that was going on. It was, she said, as if her head was awake but nothing else. Is there such a thing as a partial out-of-body experience?

I've invited my cousin, Teresa, to come for Christmas with Greg and Janina. She's thinking about it. I've invited her for the full week but I doubt she'll come for that long. I'd like it if she would. It would help with the loneliness when Guy's gone to Quebec City over New Year's Eve 2000.

It won't be easy for Guy and I to be apart on this eve of the new millenium even though it's not technically the new millenium until 2001. Not that we do anything much on New Year's Eve, we don't. It will just be unfamiliar in a long relationship where comfort is in the familiar. I'll go to early mass with my daughter-in-law, Debbie. I'm pretending to be blasé about the Y2K hullabaloo. People are going crazy buying up all kinds of stuff, including the expensive generators I've seen for sale at Canadian Tire. I won't go that far though I know I'm nervous. I just won't let on or let it get me down. The fear-mongering media disgusts me.

November 24, 1999

Charlotte, Rob's Mom and a friend of Gerry and Nathalie were all at the hospital last night when Guy arrived. Nathalie needed platelets but the endless search for a vein ended in abandonment. All her veins had collapsed. Finally they were able to put the needle on the soft part of the palm below the thumb.

Guy said it's okay to cry when you're hurting. Nathalie put her index finger against her right temple and pulled the imaginary trigger. Guy knows all about the pain of cancer. Now he knows the helplessness of the caregiver too.

The doctor has said there isn't likely to be any chemotherapy on December 6th as originally planned. Nat wants to go home then and looking at Germaine the doctor agreed. But Germaine feels that in fact the doctor was saying that it isn't going to happen. Nathalie will not leave the hospital – alive. It was the way the doctor looked at Germaine that convinced her.

Guy was very emotional last night but tried to hide it. The family stoicism. I encouraged him to talk about 'it' taking my own advice to Germaine but except to recall to the best of his ability what happened at the hospital he didn't.

Talking with Jeannie on the phone last night I told her I wasn't sure what was happening to me. Up until now I've usually wanted to go to the hospital sometimes even more than Guy, but I've come to the point where I don't want to sit in the room anymore. I'm gearing up to going and being in the Atrium working on my course. This feels safe to me. I don't have to worry that I'll burst out crying. I'm afraid I'll say something that will let Nat know that I know the truth. I keep wondering if I'm going to be given the opportunity to ask her that question, "Do you want to talk about it?" and how much I want to be given this chance. No matter the answer. Until now I hadn't realized I've asked her already! I don't know how I expected her to respond. She spoke about living with the disease for the rest of her life, on and off.

Am I avoiding my own pain? I'd like to be strong enough to face and even embrace it but I know I need time to build up my reserve of strength in order to go even a few days throughout the week. I never want to be left alone with Nat in the room again.

I'm afraid. I'm afraid of losing control.

I would like to tell Germaine how I feel but I find myself unable to do so. Perhaps this is just as well because she has enough to deal with without being burdened with my grief. I would tell her IF I were certain I could do so without being a burden. Perhaps I'll just pray for the inner strength, with God's help, to be able to be honest with her. This seemed more possible, somehow, when I was visiting nearly every day. I'm getting the sense that Germaine actually misses me.

My piece on Art Roth is scheduled to be in the *Windsor Star* on December 24th. I'm pleased as it was something I took upon myself to do and the *Star* picked up on its newsworthiness. I've given thought to enrolling in a creative writing course at the university.

My master gardener mentor told me I'm a good writer!

November 25, 1999

They've been able to remove the IV from Nat's palm and move it farther up her arm. This simple act has lifted Nat's spirit. I'm reminded of some beautiful stationery I have which says, 'Delight in the Little Things'. Nathalie's so delighted to have her hand freed up. When Guy arrived Gerry was asleep in his window chair. Nat was lying with her head at the foot of the bed. She took Guy's hand placing it on her forehead and sighed. She's been running a 40 degree Celsius temperature for several days.

She has a fungus in her blood! The medication given to her caused such a violent reaction that her body began to tremble severely.

Guy said he gets the impression that Nat gets irritated with her father. I told him that was a child's privilege. Certainly it's commonplace. I reminded myself and Guy that he wasn't present during the touching scene with Nat and her Dad in order to know that love beats irritation every time.

Nat slept last night while Guy read his book. He stayed later than usual. Guy is so like his father who visited with him in 1983 when Guy was in hospital with cancer. Both with a quiet, restful presence placing no demands or expectations on the patient. I do wish I could be that way!

Germaine doesn't stay overnight and hasn't now for some time. She's there all day. It seems to be working.

Guy and I or at least I will go up tonight. Hopefully I'll get to be in the Atrium working on my studies. I'm a selfish person wanting to do what I want. Guy is much more loving and giving. Always has been.

Nathalie can't stand the smell of coffee.

November 26, 1999

Christmas is coming and with it the obligatory shopping. Our hospital visit last night was short, just an hour and 15 minutes. We went to buy toys for our grandchildren at Toy R Us. A jigsaw puzzle for Matthew. Two for Guy and I and only if he's a good boy! I always buy a family game and this year I bought 'Chicken Soup for the Soul'. Funny I'd spend the money on the game but won't touch the books! I resent the millions which must have been made on the dozens of 'for the soul' books. It's obscene.

Tonight is a repeat. Gerry's in Nat's dark room. The television's on. Nat is lying with her head at the foot of the bed. Gerry's fanning her with a magazine. She's still running a fever. Germaine and Gerry didn't want to ask for a fan since they'd had so much trouble with the hospital when they asked for a humidifier. Apparently an engineer came into the room to check on it! Are they afraid of potential fires? Lawsuits?

I put my hands on Nat's forehead. She sighed with relief at their coolness. But it wasn't long before they felt damp and uncomfortable to her. I sat in a chair at the foot of the bed. Nat moved back to the head. When we said we wouldn't be staying long she seemed upset, "You're not leaving already are you?" She said this again as we were leaving.

Perhaps Nathalie hasn't said goodbye to me?

Nathalie's vein collapsed and the needle had to be moved to her other arm. This is an ordeal for her as the nurses search for a viable vein. Nat is in terror the entire time.

Guy asked Germaine on the phone last night if Nathalie were told she was dying what does Germaine think would happen? Germaine said Nathalie would let go and be gone the next day!

Even this poignant response from a mother doesn't stop me from feeling angry that they don't tell her. Why don't the doctors? She's an adult and has the right to know. I don't agree with Germaine that she'd let go immediately and even if she's absolutely right that still isn't a good enough reason to deny her the truth.

I spent a few moments fanning her with a magazine. She looked up at me and said she didn't want to trouble me or make me do anything I didn't want to do. I reassured her I didn't do anything I didn't want to do! I don't know if she was convinced.

It's a curious thing. I'm able to deal with whatever comes up at the hospital. Not as well as I'd like, read perfectly, but appropriately. It's when I'm at home that I get upset with what I don't like. About what I would call the duplicity.

Although this was Rob's night he didn't show. This is upsetting as we've come to rely on him to be there Mondays and Thursdays. When he's at the hospital we feel okay about taking a night off without guilt.

We don't want to let Germaine down.

Tonight Germaine is spending the night.

The telephone rang after Guy and I had gone to bed. It

was our son, Blake. Debbie, Blake's wife, had told him about Nathalie and he was genuinely concerned. We spoke for quite a while. He told me about giving blood and platelets. He wondered if the hospital had this particular machine on hand for just such a purpose. Was he thinking of giving his blood? Platelets?

I know he was.

Blake wanted to go and visit Nathalie with the children. He has only met her a few times and doesn't really know her very well. But I sensed he wanted to do something to help and support Guy. Of all our children he's the most supportive. I do think if we were in a relationship with Lynda she would be too. Greg seems more aloof.

November 27, 1999

Went to the hospital around 7 p.m. last night and left at 8:30. Gerry was there when we arrived. Nathalie has had her hair cut off since it's started falling out again. She looked like a survivor of a Nazi concentration camp. She'd look better if they could have shaved her head but she can't bear to have her scalp touched. It's so tender.

We chatted together. I told Nat if she was looking for a deep, philosophical discussion to have Guy come and get me. I'd be in the Atrium, my haven. My safe place. I'd be studying to finish both my second and final assignment of Horticulture II.

Things are about the same. Nat was sick to her stomach. She's not taking in much nourishment though her parents keep trying to find food which might please her. She's feverish still and getting something through an IV. Her shunt can't be removed because she's too weak to survive the surgery a removal would require.

What's it feel like to have a foreign object in your chest?

As the vigil continues I become less and less inclined to visit the hospital. I don't mind staying in the Atrium studying. I just don't want to be in Nathalie's room. It's never been easy for me but it's getting worse every day. Guy is wonderful sitting quietly with Nat, each of them gently stroking the top of the other's head in their farewell ritual. A sweet, tender gesture.

I wrote a letter to Lynda yesterday and felt a burden lift from my heart. I want to write more letters to her. I won't mail them. I'll put them in a box for safekeeping for her.

I hope I die before she does.

Guy, Debbie and Matthew, our grandson, are going to the Santa Claus parade tonight.

December 1, 1999

We haven't seen Nathalie for several days. Germaine called saying she hasn't wanted visitors. I can't go tonight. Guy might go. A nurse told Germaine she doesn't know what they'll do when they run out of veins. Nat has asked the nurses what it's like in the hospital at Christmas time.

Monday and Tuesday nights Guy and I had been ready to leave for the hospital when Germaine called to say not to go. We try hard not to take this personally. Why can't I take it in that she's said goodbye to me?

December 2, 1999

The Music Express concert, 'The Call of Christmas' was a welcome release from the hospital routine. When we got home Guy called Germaine. She said that Nat has had several very bad days. She's vomiting a lot. So much that they almost lost her yesterday. She's receiving platelets. The doctor has told Germaine that Nat might simply slip into a coma. This often happens when someone is terminally ill.

No extraordinary measures will be taken.

The doctor knows.

Charlotte came up last night with her two younger sons, Andrew and Alex and though Nathalie had wanted to see them she was no longer strong enough. A friend from the French Club also visited. After five minutes Nat asked for her Mom. Nat wants only her Mom and Dad now.

Guy's going to ask Germaine if there's anything we can do

to help. Practical help like cleaning the house or preparing food. Gerry goes up to the hospital right at the end of day shift staying until 10:30 p.m. or later. Germaine goes in the mornings around 10 a.m. staying until about 9 p.m. She didn't stay overnight last night.

We feel the nearness of death. I wish there were some way to help Nathalie deal with her fear. It's hard sometimes to keep in mind that there is much happening in the room when we're not there. A few hours, even every day, isn't much when taken in context.

Christmas is still on Nat's mind; she is asking again to go home. Just to be with her immediate family. This seems unlikely. I hope she doesn't die on my birthday, December 16th, or on Christmas Day. If she does those days will never be the same again for me or her family or for Nathalie's Aunt Nicole who shares my birthday.

I would like to see Nathalie again before she slips into a coma but my intuition tells me it's not going to happen. I miss her already. I wish I'd have stayed with her when I had the chance. It just seemed that she might live for quite a while and there wasn't any urgency.

I have grown to love Nathalie unconditionally.

Once I believed I wasn't capable of loving anyone. I was wrong.

Nathalie is such a lovely young woman. So unique. An original. Artistic and beautiful. And funny. And brave.

Born just before Guy and I married, she was the reason Germaine didn't come to our wedding. I didn't take to her as a child. She was rather homely and gangly. All arms and legs. As she grew into young womanhood she grew tall and beautiful with an aquiline nose, a maternal gene, hands with long tapering fingers and gorgeous chestnut hair, more dark brown than red.

Nathalie travelled to England alone when a planned trip with her friend, Sammi*, didn't materialize. Nathalie never held it against her friend for not following through with their plans to go overseas as a twosome.

Germaine hasn't been able to forgive Sammi. Germaine said Sammi was like a daughter to her. Germaine's anger often fueled her during the time with Nathalie and this disease. When Sammi came to visit Nat in the hospital she wouldn't stay around or in the room if Germaine was present. Nathalie protected Sammi from her mother's hurt wrath asking her mother not to be in the room when Sammi was due. Nathalie's loyalty upset Germaine but she acquiesced.

December 3, 1999

Lynda is 39 years old today.

Guy and Nathalie spent the evening in her room. She showed him her arm covered with huge bruises.

Where does the blood go they keep giving her?

She told Guy about how she met Rob. She and a bunch of her friends were in a bar. Rob was off on the sidelines. She approached him. She said she knew instinctively he wouldn't approach her. I knew a man like that a long time ago. He would sit in a bar by himself quietly drinking a beer. Before long there'd be a woman at his table. He talked with his eyes.

This kind of man can be irresistible to women.

Guy said Nat told him she'd be going home in a week for Christmas and getting more chemo in January. Martin called the room while Guy was there, looking for his parents. No one knew where they were.

I hope for a moment they were able to forget.

Did Gerry go through with his plans to arrange Nat's funeral? Guy and I were closer to Germaine and Gerry the first week Nathalie was in hospital. As time passes we grow apart with longer spaces between seeing each other.

Life goes on.

Christmas is coming.

There is so much to do and so little desire to do anything except keep the vigil. Yet it's as if because Nathalie hasn't died yet or didn't die right away then everyone goes back to the more mundane routine of daily living.

Nathalie told Guy she has two friends her parents,

especially Germaine, don't like. She doesn't let that stop her from seeing them as she likes them very much.

I can see the look of determination on her face.

At Germaine's house last night, after mass and dinner, I was conscious of listening. I'm aware I'm a sounding board where Germaine can come and talk about whatever is on her mind at any moment. I'm there as much as is possible, without judgement, knowing that I may be the only person with whom she can be herself, completely.

Nathalie's friend, Sammi, was uppermost in Germaine's mind. Sammi had hurt Nathalie by backing out of the trip to Europe at the last minute, causing Germaine and Gerry to lose a large deposit. Sammi was cruel to Nathalie but in particular she was nasty when speaking about Germaine and Gerry. I don't recall what she said but she has never had the grace to apologize nor has she repaid Germaine the deposit. Germaine once looked upon Sammi as a daughter, making her actions that much more hurtful. Now the sight of her or the mention of her name is unbearable.

Elaborate arrangements are made to facilitate her visits to Nat in hospital.

When Germaine speaks about Sammi she becomes very angry and animated. I think it's good for her to have a target for her anger. She's able to laugh and is very expressive. It shows me a side I've never been invited to look at before now and makes my relationship with her more intimate. If Sammi had the sense to come and say she's sorry to Germaine, even without repaying the money, Germaine would forgive her immediately.

Nathalie was placed on the critical list last week. On Wednesday, December 1st she was coughing and vomiting so much that the doctors and nurses felt she was going to die. Germaine had great difficulty finding the words to describe Nat's colour to me. After several moments she said, "Grey". I've never heard this before but Germaine said that when someone was close to death the nose turns white! Nat's nose turned white, for a while.

Nat hasn't wanted her bed sheets changed for close to a week. She hasn't had a shower or sponge bath, even her clothes haven't been changed. This has upset Germaine's aesthetic sense. Finally all of the above has been done and she's feeling much better.

Nathalie's body is retaining fluid. Edema is evident in her ankles, legs and feet as well as in her back around her kidney. Germaine was shocked the first time she saw it.

Hesitantly I asked where all the platelets went since Nat is having them every day now. Apparently the blood turns to water! Nat's white blood count has to drop to about 13 in order for her to have the platelets. A normal person has hundreds of platelets. Her red blood count is nearly non-existent. In other words she's barely alive. She's not on oxygen though the doctors want her on it.

She's still saying she's coming home for Christmas Day. It seems that the nearness of Christmas and her love of it keep Nat going. Marty has begun to decorate the house. The tree is up and ornaments grace its boughs. The living room is filled with dozens of Christmas boxes hauled upstairs for this, usually joyous occasion.

The house feels cold, empty. I'd offer to clean it for Germaine but I still don't feel it's my place. But I still should offer. Martin's there in the day time and could show me where stuff is.

I don't really think Nathalie will be home for Christmas or ever again but I think it's really important that someone in the family decorate for Christmas anyway. If Nat dies before Christmas and the house isn't decorated they may never be able to do it again.

Germaine was mulling over what she would have to eat should Nat come home for Christmas Day. It would have to be things like cold cuts. Nat can't stand the smell of food – it makes her sick – so the traditional French Canadian Tortiere and other warm things, even coffee, are out of the question.

Chantal is having some problems with her pregnancy. She's experiencing some pain. Stress from the grief of Nat's illness is the doctor's diagnosis. I hope everything works out well.

Gerry is spending more and more time at the hospital. There seemed to be some mix-up on Wednesday night. Guy spoke to Gerry on the phone as he always speaks to either him or Germaine. Guy said he would go to the hospital from 7 to 9 p.m. and Gerry agreed. However just a few moments after Guy had hung up the phone Gerry called back and said he was going to the hospital instead of waiting until later so Guy wouldn't have to go.

Germaine had a slightly different version of this event believing, incorrectly, that Guy wasn't able to go. This was either just a miscommunication between her and her husband or else Gerry deliberately led her to believe that Guy wasn't coming for reasons unknown to anyone except Gerry.

Perhaps not even to him?

I finally got up my courage and told Germaine, last night, that I believe Nat said goodbye to me several weeks ago on that Sunday in November. Germaine said Nat tells her and Gerry how very much she loves them, not in the least shy about expressing her feelings.

I wonder if she's told her Mom about having the out-of-body experience (near death?) when she was in Toronto?

December 7, 1999

Guy went to the hospital last night for two hours. Nathalie has to be helped out of bed to go to the washroom. They've forbidden her to get out of bed alone. They are still giving her platelets.

Why?

If they stopped giving her blood would she die faster?

She barely talks anymore. Her mouth is full of sores both inside and outside. For the first time Guy felt, too, that she was yellow, though Germaine says to her knowledge there is no liver involvement but rather it is the blood. Does she have Non-Hodgkins Lymphoma? Do we have lymph glands all over our body?

I want all measures to be stopped. I wish Nathalie knew

about how close she is to death. Does she know? How can someone not know? I find myself getting angry. I hope I never have to go through this sad process with one of my children.

Guy sits in the rocker up close to Nathalie's head. Gerry sits back in the corner watching television. I sit in the Atrium working on my course chatting with whomever wants to chat. Marty and Rob come to the hospital when they can. It's Germaine whose vigil never ends. Even at home she doesn't rest, her mind, heart and soul with her baby daughter.

Guy and I find ourselves passing judgement. How easy it is to judge and not to own the feelings which the judgement covers up. We aren't watching our youngest child die, helpless to stop death's inevitability. We aren't so exhausted we put our own health in jeopardy. If we become tired we can stay home, rest up and choose when we'll visit the hospital again.

Nathalie is not our child.

Yet even in the light of this understanding we still find ourselves being judgemental. I've offered to help Germaine any numbers of times – driving to Toronto with her and Nat when Nat had to go there for the bone marrow replacement not to mention the innumerable visits before and after. I've offered my general help, too. Gerry asked me to drive him home from the hospital one day. Germaine intervened and said she would.

My reading this morning in Sheldon Kopp's book, 'The Blues Ain't Nothing But a Good Soul Feeling Bad' spoke about refusing help when it's offered. How rejected the person offering the help feels. How some people martyr themselves feeling this makes them 'look good' instead of accepting the help of people who care about them. This is exactly how I feel. It might even be beneath the fact that I won't offer to clean the house or cook meals for them. I am still angry at Germaine's refusal of my help in the past and this is a way for me to act out my anger toward them. I tell myself that they can afford a housekeeper to clean the house and their neighbour will cook them whatever they ask for.

I'm a big baby.

We don't think Nathalie will live much longer. We don't

think she'll make it to Christmas but then what do we know?

I talked again with Jeannie and she told me of different people with whom she's volunteered. The man who was dying of AIDS was able to get out of bed and into a wheelchair until just a few days before he died. He could also toilet himself. Jeannie said this was so important to him as he didn't want anyone else to have to take care of his personal hygiene.

I remember my friend's Mom having to be taken to the washroom and how hard my friend found this to do. Her Mom didn't live too long afterward. No more than a few weeks.

It snowed yesterday for the first time this winter. A heavy wet snow bending the branches of the *Cornus Alba var.* 'Variegated Dogwood' planted in Dad's memory. It was the kind of snow that doesn't last because it's not cold enough yet.

I've begun putting up decorations as well as sorting through them discarding things that I haven't used for a few years. I've also been sorting papers in my room. It's an onerous task made bearable by doing a few minutes at a time rather than tackling the entire job in one go-round.

At Christmas I feel my sorrow at the lack of closeness in my family and I long for it to be different. We have so few close friends. We don't do the things we think other families take joy in at Christmas time. We're planning to go to our American friends' home this weekend.

December 8, 1999

Guy left for the hospital last night just after 7 but not before we played a game of cards. I was in my room at the computer hoping to spend an hour on my studies when the phone rang. It was Guy telling me that Nathalie had taken a turn for the worse. Chantal was on her way from out-of-town. Marty, Germaine and Gerry were at the hospital. Did I want to come to the hospital?

I did.

When we arrived at Nat's room, not sure what to expect, she was sitting up in bed an oxygen mask covering her nose and mouth held securely in place by an ugly green strap. Rob had joined the throng.

Stoned out of her mind on the three musketeers, Morphine, Dilaudid and Adivan, Nat was talking a mile a minute her eyes rolling back in her head. She would look at us with her eyes wide open as if startled to find herself in a room filled with people. Most of what she said was incoherent to everybody except Martin. The scene between brother and sister reminded me of a mother with a toddler just learning to talk. The mother alone understands what her child is saying and she translates for everyone else. Though Nathalie was often out of it she had many moments of lucidity. Most of all she was extraordinarily funny cracking jokes and generally being hilarious. We were all laughing. It felt so good.

Nathalie told us she was seeing double. The room was very crowded indeed.

The talking was light but I wished from time to time that everyone would just be quiet. We were when Nat 'left' us for a while. Her mouth was very dry because of the oxygen. She had a few drinks of water. Her body seemed blue to me and it's obvious she's covered with bruises. She was being given antibiotics by IV and she's still giving herself the needle to try to keep her white blood count up.

When we left Nathalie's room we convened in the ground floor cafeteria. I asked questions; Germaine answered. Guy and Gerry remained largely silent.

Nat had taken a bad turn today after going to the washroom. Germaine told Guy that her bowel movement is all different colours as if she's shitting her body down the toilet. It was at this point that they upped everything including the oxygen to 100% as well as the strong narcotic, Dilaudid. I think Adivan is for anxiety. I remember one of my clients taking it occasionally when she'd get upset.

Germaine's been invited to have Nat moved to a larger room in the Palliative Care area on 4 Main. A Christmas Party for Nathalie has been suggested to be held in the Atrium. Germaine doesn't know what to do about these suggestions. She doesn't seem to want either.

Ask Nathalie?

I know how hard all these different decisions are for Germaine. How much as a mother she doesn't see her daughter as an adult but as a little child dependent upon her for everything. I remember feeling this way when my son was in trouble. I wanted to wrap him up in a blanket and cradle him in my arms.

He was a grown man.

Gerry still hasn't made funeral arrangements as he'd considered. I don't think anything will happen until Nat's dead.

Germaine doesn't know what to do about the ring Nat bought for Rob. It's engraved inside with Nat's thanks. Her Christmas present for him.

Germaine is terrified of doing something which will cause Nat to hate her and which Germaine will regret when Nat's dead. I said as clearly as I could that they would have nothing to regret. They've done everything parents could do for their child. They've given Nathalie a profound love.

Germaine said she supposed her family was too private. This was in response to something I'd said about the family. I think this is true but it's more a kind of exclusivity. Insularity? Is there such a word? Only certain people are invited into the family's inner circle. They are very selective.

Aren't we all?

Chantal and Darrin arrived looking disheveled. It was sweet to see Darrin's solicitude toward Chantal, bringing her a glass of water. The pregnancy is beginning to show and she moaned several times about the car trip to Windsor. It can't be much fun for these two young people on the one hand looking forward to the birth of their first child and the anticipatory grief of Nat's imminent death. I think of how a gardener feels every late fall/early winter as the garden dies back into the earth. Even though one knows the cycle completes itself in this way before awakening in the spring with new life. Life and death are part of a circle, each one necessary to the other. The glaring difference between watching Nathalie die and watching a garden die is that a garden will come back to life again. Nathalie will too but we won't see her until we ourselves follow her into death.

Guy and I are more and more on the sidelines as the immediate family comes together as if into one indivisible entity. Just as when people are thrown into a situation unfamiliar to them some come out stronger, more refined like iron put through the fire before turning into steel. This is happening to Marty. It's he who understands Nathalie's symbolic language. It's Marty who helps Nathalie when she has to cough. The young man I once looked upon as a poster boy for a man's formal wear shop is not just another pretty face. He has a depth of kindness and humour that seems to becoming more apparent as he walks closely with his little sister.

Nathalie doesn't like it when she realizes that Rob has left her room. Her eyes open in what seems to be terror and she'll ask after him. She's at peace when he's there. It's heartbreaking to see these two young people in this difficult situation. They've broken up a few times yet today they're together in a powerful way. Rob comes to the hospital whenever he can.

Something else is happening in her room. It's becoming a holy place. There's a kind of sacredness amid all the stuff – flowers, teddy bears, clothes, coats, purses, drink bottles, IV stands and tubes, hospital bed, a bunch of chairs, a commode and bedside stand. There's a palpable serenity. Suffering is holding hands with love. So much so that I wonder to myself if we won't want to keep coming back to this room even when Nathalie's no longer in it?

I've finally come to see the futility of asking the unanswerable 'why'? There is no answer to this question. It isn't even actually the question is it? Perhaps the question is rather, 'How'? How do we live in the face of life's apparent randomness. What do we learn from the suffering of this young woman? I wonder if some of what we can learn is the importance of making friends with our feelings. The willingness to share our feelings with others. The importance of being positive and resilient without being facile or superficial. Like letting your heart break wide open without being sentimental, maudlin or melodramatic. The absolute priority of love with everything implicit in its meaning. Painters, writers, poets, musicians have spent lifetimes endeavouring to plumb the topic and yet its power to heal even the most wounded soul remains a mystery.

I recall a morning in my small garden on Caroline Street. It's spring and I chance, out of my peripheral vision, to see the Cosmos swaying in the gentle morning air. Like dancers on point, their faces bathed in the warmth of the early sun's embrace. My heart skipped a beat, my breath caught, as I was swept back in time to mid winter the day I planted the minuscule seeds in a black, plastic nine cell pack with moistened soil-less mix. I placed a see-through plastic top on the larger tray and put it on top of the refrigerator. The 70 degree heat generated by the refrigerator's motor just warm enough to germinate the seeds.

Seeds give no indication of the glory they'll display when in full flower. Tiny ugly, shriveled up, misshapen, they look more like tiny bird droppings than a vessel pregnant with fragile beauty.

I thought about St. John of the Cross and his dark night of the soul. This journey is like the seed which must go through a period where it lives in the darkness of the earth, unseen by the human eye. Once the seed is planted the gardener must let go and leave the results in the hands of the Creator.

I'm relying more and more on Jeannie and her experience with the dying. I spoke with her several times yesterday. I told her this journal is much more than the process of Nat's journey bringing her to death. It's the story of Lynda's estrangement from me and the pain of a relationship thrown away by her because she thinks she didn't get what she wanted from me. It's about Guy and his grief over the loss of his parents, especially his Mom. It's about respecting human life and honouring a person's right to make mistakes. It's about Nathalie, and others, being given the choice over their own life right up to the end including choosing to be in denial! It's about learning to flow with life rather than fight it or attempt to control what's out of our hands. It's about truth and integrity as well as sensitivity, restraint, patience and modesty. It's about listening and biting your tongue. It's about not being critical but being understanding and accepting of each individual's way of dealing with things at their own level of consciousness.

This is not only difficult for me, it's difficult for most of us.

Last night as we were falling asleep Guy told me he loved me. He hasn't said that for a very long time. I knew it arose out of the way I was with Nat, his family and him last night. I thanked him for his love.

I love him too.

December 9, 1999

Guy went to the hospital last night while I went to the Scottish Club. Alistair MacLeod was reading from his first novel, 'No Great Mischief'. I purchased two of the books – autographed. One for me and one for Kate, a Christmas gift for her husband. I had the book gift-wrapped.

Dr. MacLeod is such an unaffected man. He seems shy though his wife, Anita, says he's not. He seems kind. I wonder if he is? His superb writing tells of the dark, sad side of life and its waste. The piece he read was about the protagonist going as a young man to Toronto to meet with his brother, an alcoholic, who lives in a rooming house. He paints a visual picture with his words, rich in pathos and love. I can't wait to read the book. Yet at the same time I want simply to hold it and touch it before I reach inside of it. It took him more than ten years to complete. I want to take my time honouring the time he took in the writing.

Though not as high as she was the other night, Nat wasn't saying very much. Rob was alone with her. Chantal and Germaine were at home. Gerry spent most of the evening with Guy in the Atrium. The doctors are saying she won't live beyond the weekend. I can't decide what to do about our planned trip to visit our American friends. I really don't want to go. Once again I'd be doing it for Guy because he expressed an interest in visiting them.

My friend, Kate, just told me that doctors base their predictions about impending death upon a person's vital signs. Nat's breathing is shallow; her heart rate fast. She's not receiving platelets. Just one IV now. She's not eating, just drinking, water, Sprite or Ginger Ale.

I've wondered about writing about Nat as if I were her. I'm not sure I've written much in the first person except factual material. I usually write fiction as the omniscient narrator. What would it be like to write as if I'm stoned on drugs to blot out my body's pain? What would it be like to write as if I were 24 years old and dying?

December 10, 1999

When Guy and I went to the hospital last night Rob and Gerry were in the room. Nat was sleeping when we arrived and for the first time I really saw how thin she was. Her head was turned to the right revealing her profile in sharp relief. Her long slim neck seemed to announce her thinness.

A quiet presence, Rob is now coming every night, staying last night until 9 o'clock. I went into the Atrium and began working. I was enjoying myself for nearly an hour when a gentleman joined me.

He asked me if I was taking care of some paperwork. I told him I was studying to become a master gardener. He became animated referring to the plants in the room, asking me about the ones whose leaves were tipped with brown. What did I think was wrong with them? I told him it could be any number of things including inadequate light, although I couldn't be sure since I haven't been in the Atrium during the day, over or under watering or insufficient nourishment. I pointed out to him that the *Ficus Benjamina* 'Weeping Fig' appeared to be doing well, even flourishing, in spite of someone putting Plant Shine on its leaves which clogs up the leaves' pores, harming rather than helping it. In fact, Plant Shine if used continuously can kill a plant. It's kind of like someone who keeps using pesticides in the garden and wonders why they are never free of pests.

Tom* is from the county. He is suffering from acute leukemia, in hospital for another round of chemotherapy. His soft, white hair is scant and stands on end looking as if he'd stuck a finger in a light socket. An extrovert, he began to tell me of his calls to various politicians about the terrible state of the air outside the Atrium. He continued for several moments pulling names out of a hat – Susan Whelan, MP for Essex, the staff at Bruce Crozier's office. A farmer, Tom was determined to find out what could be done about the stench he'd encountered earlier in the day. I asked him if he'd forgotten that Windsor is the most polluted city in Canada? I don't think he heard me. Though gravely ill Tom still had the clout to make elected members of parliaments or councils pay attention to his concerns. Did he still need to feel he was a productive member of the community who could 'get things done' when people heard his name – his voice? Is this the way someone as ill as Tom hangs on to what control he has? It makes sense to me.

Tom is a devout Roman Catholic. At the end of a chain hanging around his neck was an unusual crucifix. It wasn't shiny enough to be sterling silver. Pewter?

He went on to tell me of the people he knew in the hospital, calling them by name and detailing some of their illnesses, all cancers. He told me of asking for prayers through a prayer chain. Like a chain letter, sort of, but hopefully more effective, he said thoughtfully.

Carrying his scarf and hat against the winter night and walking with a distinctive cane, Tom, in his checkered flannel shirt, was an unlikely angel of mercy. Yet I sensed his positive spirit brought hope to those he blessed with his presence.

I enjoyed our time together and as he took leave of me to have another 'blast of poison' he took my small hand in his still strong, gnarled one and wished me well, thanking me for the time we'd spent together.

Tom had just slipped out the door when Germaine arrived looking refreshed albeit very tired. Her hair looking newly washed. Had she coloured it too? She's white underneath the chemically created auburn. I'd love to see her hair in its natural state. She sat down heavily in one of the rattan chairs and immediately began to talk.

She said that Nat had soaked her bed during the night and this embarrassed her. An air mattress has been put on the bed to aid in preventing bed sores. Nat's body is very cold now. Guy had spoken about this earlier as well as commenting on the change in her breathing – short, high breaths with long pauses as opposed to the quick, short ones close together that she had been experiencing. Apparently her breathing changes depending upon the medication she's been given.

"I don't think she'll pass the night," Guy said. "Her breathing is just like my Mom's shortly before she died. Very shortly before."

However later in the evening when Nathalie's breathing returned to the short quick breaths Guy changed his mind.

Germaine doesn't want Nat moved to the Palliative Care room though it's a larger space. Is there a window in that room? Nor does she want a Christmas party for her before Christmas. Nat is still saying she's going home for Christmas and even asking the doctors if she can go home. She keeps repeating that she's going home for Christmas. For the first time this morning I realized that Nat is speaking the symbolic language used by the dying. It's her way of telling us she'll be gone by Christmas. Is she asking the doctors to let her go? Guy doesn't think so. He feels she was referring to being in her own room, her own bed. But I know the importance of not taking everything the dying person says literally. The symbolism is there and we need to look beyond and beneath the obvious. We need to read between the lines. We need to learn the language.

Nathalie asked Germaine again during the night, "Mom, do you feel sorry for me?"

Chantal and Darrin will stay until this weekend. Guy still thinks Nat won't live beyond it. But then in the next moment he'll shake his head saying that Nathalie continues to surprise, even startle. Whereas one minute it seems she won't live another moment or just a few moments longer, this can change so that once again we are thrown back into the unknown. Where Nat's fate, like the fate of everyone, is out of our hands. As we seek to make sense or grasp control we feel it float away like the wisp of a dandelion seed whispering to a spring wind.

We're the same, aren't we? Here for an instant and then gone forever but not forgotten as long as we are loved. When we are loved we live on in the memory of the one who loves us. So we never die.

How I long to be able to sit quietly with Nat and have her tell me if she's having any supernatural experiences; out-of-body or near death experiences. How I wish she could clear up the mystery behind the veil. Has she been privileged already to step through – to catch a glimpse of the other side? Are there angels waiting to take her hand and lead her into Paradise? Are her grandparents nearby? Do they wait on the other side of the river that separates life and death? Is there a bridge Nat must cross when she finally leaves us never to return?

Or like the line in Hamlet, will "flights of angels sing thee to thy rest"?

I'd like to believe that those who have died and who love her and whom she loves are getting ready to welcome her home. They are preparing her room.

December 11, 1999
Guy and I went to the hospital last night just before 7 staying until well after 10 p.m. Darrin and Chantal left shortly after we arrived.

Nathalie had had an exciting day. She was given her own graduation from St. Clair College complete with a three year honours diploma in Advertising – Business, represented by a green velvet scarf trimmed in gold. She wore a corsage of red carnations. Two helium balloons – one really striking in gold with black lettering, 'Congratulations Graduate' and another rainbow coloured one – were floating beneath the ceiling of her room. A computer-generated banner 'Congratulations Nathalie' with a graduate's cap and diploma on it flew behind the television set.

Two of Nat's favourite teachers were present to celebrate the occasion. A number of nurses were there as well as Gerry, Germaine, Marty, Darrin, Chantal, Rob and his mother, Charlotte, his father, Andrew and Alex, his brothers and Katherine, his sister. Nathalie speaks with affection of his sister. Rob's background is Italian and Scottish. He favours his Celtic ancestors with his wheat coloured hair and skin.

Nathalie had been given a video of the ceremony.

Germaine and Gerry, though maintaining their composure, are clearly moved - the imperative 'don't cry' holding throughout the presentation. Nathalie was reclining on a long wheelchair fully equipped with oxygen mask, ugly green rubber strap encircling the top of her balding head. The disease grinning its demonic grasp.

I could barely keep from crying out, what's it like to see yourself when you are so sick—so close to death? What face looks back at you?

Naturally I didn't say a word.

I asked Nathalie if she was afraid. Immediately she became guarded and defensive.

"About what?" she said.

"Oh, just anything at all".

"No!" she said sharply.

Talking with Jeannie this morning she said something I hope I don't forget. If I'm ever in the same place as Nathalie I can be open to hearing the truth. I can let other people know I know the truth. I can let them know they don't have to pretend that everything's fine. I can let them know that I may not have long to live but that I'm alive right now. I can ask them not to treat me as if I'm already dead. If I can acknowledge the truth it will free me to make as many decisions about my life as possible while I still have the emotional and mental capacity.

But then, it's so easy to talk about what I'd like to happen. If put in the same situation how can I ever know how I'll react or respond to 'the truth'. Can one ever know?

I do know that it must be nearly unbearable to watch your child die. I can't begin to know what this is like since I've never gone through it.

Germaine wasn't feeling well when we went down together with Gerry to the cafeteria. She felt hot all over and she was sweating. She was going home to spend the night. Gerry was staying at the hospital. I heard the nurse tell them that Nathalie's vital signs were stable.

The nurses have refused to give Nathalie any more needles because it is a form of torture. Nat thinks they will continue after giving her a little break.

Nathalie says she's going home for Christmas.

Guy is now visiting five people on 4th North including a Scouter, a fellow from work and two others I don't know. Last night Guy's friend showed up and together they went to visit the Scouter staying quite late.

I continued working on my studies in the Atrium. Tom came in again. We chatted for a few moments. I found myself trying not to be available to him. He wandered out onto the roof to have a few puffs from his pipe. Earlier, he'd had a visitor who played the fiddle for him. I'd found it rather annoying. Tom, on the other hand, was deeply appreciative, telling me how much he loved the fiddle.

As I sit quietly in the Atrium, taking a break from my reading, I found myself wanting to be with Nathalie. But the thought of it makes me so uncomfortable, too. What if she needs something from me I can't give?

In spite of my fear I return to her room. I watched her as she spent a considerable time deciding about getting a drink. She was finally able and was well enough and awake enough to watch television. I asked her if she was in any pain. She said the pain was all in her face. She kept stretching her lips over her teeth.

Guy told me he, too, wanted to ask Nathalie what it felt like to see herself on the graduation video.

I don't feel quite like such a freak.

Today Guy is at Ford's Children's Christmas party. He took Matthew. When we were grocery shopping at Zehr's early this morning he bought Matthew some knee high socks. He bought himself a pair of those tiny stretch gloves for when he walks the dogs. We were out the door at 7:15 a.m. travelling first to Zehr's then to Remark Farms and finally to the TBQ for their delicious breakfast on a skillet before Guy had to leave to pick up Matthew for the party.

Matthew can wrap Guy and I right round his tiny fingers.

Kenny, Lynda's estranged husband, and my grandson, Benjamin, will be here in the next few hours. I'm terrified to spend even this short time with them. I'm so filled with sadness I'm afraid I'll cry. I'm afraid I'll not be honest with them. I'm afraid I'll say something which will hurt Benjamin. I want to spend time alone with him. I might ask him if he'd like to go for a walk with me to see Matthew. I hope I remember to take pictures of him and Kenny. I'm afraid I'll forget.

This time of year is difficult for me. I become depressed because of the family rife. Do I need to listen to Morrie in "Tuesdays with Morrie" by Mitch Albom (Doubleday, N.Y. 1997) who said, "Forgive everyone everything."

December 14, 1999

Kenny and Benjamin were here for three hours. We had a terrific time together sitting in the dining room and just talking. Kenny looked tired and old. There's something wrong with his mouth. His upper plate doesn't appear to fit very well. He just started a new job in Toronto last Monday.

Benjamin is a delight – full of piss and vinegar. He brought me a lovely birthday card which he'd signed for me.

I'd thought Kenny would be reticent to talk about Lynda and Courtney in front of Benjamin. He wasn't. I knew it wasn't wise to speak about them in his presence but I was so hungry for news of them I wasn't wise. Lynda has moved. Benjamin told Kenny's common-law partner before he told his father. Courtney is working as a waitress. Lynda gave up her floral designer position and is tending bar full time. Lynda's partner may be working a midnight shift somewhere. Kenny didn't know.

For the most part Kenny has nothing to do with Lynda

anymore. It sounds like she has generous access to Benjamin.

Kenny kept asking me not to give up on her. He told me to practice what I preach! I think he still loves my daughter in spite of everything.

I forgot, as I was afraid I would, to take any pictures. I felt so much lighter after they hugged and kissed me goodbye, like a weight had been lifted from my heart. It's a terrible thing when children turn against their parents without trying to work things out. I can understand children of abusive parents not wanting them in their lives but most parents do the best they can with the 'light' they have. Adult children need to be more forgiving, less tied to a romantic notion of a childhood they think they should have had and didn't get! It is, after all, up to the child now grown to adulthood to deal with their past, to learn from it, to grow from it. It's now out of the hands of the parents.

I remember Dr. Havelka, my wonderful Psychology professor at King's College. He taught me a Humanities course in third year. He said a child needs to befriend his/her parent and resolve all of the issues from the past by the time they're 25 years of age. His belief was that not to do so is to remain immature emotionally and spiritually.

Guy and I went out for supper. Afterward we saw the movie, The Green Mile with Tom Hanks. I loved the movie. One of Guy's mates from work was there. We'd once given him a bunch of water hyacinths from our pond garden at the old house. He's such a lovely sweet man. But his wife is a horror. She kept calling him stupid throughout the brief moments we spent chatting with them. I wish I'd had the 'balls' to call her on it.

Last night Guy went to the hospital alone from 6:30 to 9 p.m. Germaine came back around 8:40 so she and Guy spent some time in the cafeteria.

Nathalie is receiving platelets again. Germaine doesn't know why but she's going to find out. One of Nathalie's friends was visiting her in the early part of the evening. The staff chose this time to try distracting Nathalie while they searched for a vein in her right hand.

Nicole and Micheline drove to Windsor Sunday afternoon, staying for just two hours. I found this a thoughtful thing to do.

I didn't want to go to the hospital last night. I wanted to finish some chores at home including crocheting Matthew's afghan for Christmas.

December 15, 1999

We've finished our Christmas shopping.

Guy talked to Germaine on the telephone. The reason Nathalie's being given platelets is so that she won't hemorrhage internally. They are giving her blood so that she has oxygen in her body.

I called TVO yesterday afternoon and spoke with Lance Secretan, author and public speaker. He looks like my image of a Buddhist monk. I called him to speak about unconditional love. I said that while I do attempt to practice unconditional love that I keep getting hung up on wanting to be thanked. Is this my ego, I asked? He said it was but that we needed an ego or we wouldn't get out of bed in the morning! He said that he liked and wanted to be thanked for things he did for others. He said I was being too hard on myself. (I don't know how many times I've been told this.) He said none of us is perfect and that this might be an aspect of my perfectionism.

And we've never met!

December 17, 1999

Yesterday was my 63rd birthday. Benjamin's 10th. Guy gave me a book by Gail Sheehy, 'Hillary's Choice' (Random House, N.Y. 1999) about Hillary Rodham Clinton, the First Lady of the United States. I've already begun reading it.

Guy went to the hospital last night while I went to my Woman Within group. I was leading the group. The theme I chose was 'Receiving'. A topic I thought appropriate on my birthday.

Nathalie spoke little to Guy. Guy spoke to Germaine again about telling Nathalie the truth of her dying. Germaine said the doctors and other people who have been through this have said not to tell her. Even though Nat is chronologically an adult she was only 22 when she was diagnosed. She's never lived independently, married or had children. In other words she's too young to be told the truth?

What's wrong with me that I am unable to accept that not everyone does things the way I do? What kind of ego is it that is unable to accept differences?

Jeannie helped me yet again on the telephone this morning. Her friend, a Palliative Care nurse, believes that the dying deal with death unconsciously even if they don't appear to be doing so on a conscious level. Jeannie also believes that Germaine wanting a picture of Guy and Nathalie performing their nightly ritual of farewell is a way of acknowledging her dying. And of course if Nathalie did say in her sleep, "I'm dying—I'm dying", doesn't this show she's aware of her impending death?

Germaine said Nathalie is bleeding internally but it is being kept to a minimum by the platelets. Last night she had nothing except the oxygen. She told Guy she has trouble swallowing the pills. Her mouth and lips are covered with sores. The air mattress was taken away. Nathalie found it too uncomfortable.

We really believe Nathalie will live until Christmas. Germaine is willing to bring Nathalie home because she still seems to want this. Germaine has a room now at the hospital where she can sleep as Nat has started moaning in her sleep keeping Germaine awake.

Guy explained to Germaine that he's leaving for Quebec City on the 26th. If Nat dies when he's away he will not return for the funeral unless a family member chooses to drive down and then bring him back. Graciously, Germaine said that Guy has been here while Nathalie's alive. That's more important than when she's dead. Or words to that effect.

I saw a piece on television yesterday about helping the caregiver of a dying person. It said the usual things – offer to clean the house, get the groceries, do the laundry, make a meal, sit with the dying person, encourage the caregiver to take good care of themselves including getting to their own doctor and dentist appointments as well as not forgetting to take their medications.

I know of couples where the caregiver has died before the dying person.

Guy and I will likely go to the hospital tonight.

December 18, 1999

When we went to the hospital last night and entered Nathalie's room I gasped out loud. The change in her appearance from a week ago was startling. She appeared to be resting. Her eyes were half opened; her mouth open; her lips covered with black sores caused from the application of gentian violet. I was so shocked I couldn't speak. I kept looking away from her face. I don't think she was asleep. Her eyes seemed to follow me piercing straight through me. I felt she could hear my inner thoughts. I didn't want her to know how hard it was for me to see her in this way, so different from the Nathalie of a month ago.

She was holding one of those little kidney basins as she had been vomiting during the day. Germaine says the vomit is disgusting. Nathalie is receiving something through an IV. I think she's getting oxygen through her nose but I'm not sure. They keep changing the vehicle for her to receive oxygen. She has the vaporizer going again.

It felt to me that Nathalie has passed from living her dying to dying her dying.

The room is decorated for Christmas with streamers in the doorway, a little Christmas tree with Santa Claus lights, a half dozen small stuffed teddy bears or other animals including a little lamb brought to her by a home care nurse who continues to visit her. Germaine is very grateful for her visits. There are three or four helium balloons.

Guy and I have offered our help to Germaine to get the house in order for Nathalie's possible return home on Christmas Eve. Germaine was able to vacuum a little yesterday as well as do some laundry. She said this helped her to feel better. She feels, acutely, the lack of physical movement since being Nathalie's primary caregiver leaves her moving around the room or hospital quite slowly. She would benefit from long walks every day if she could manage it.

Would she do it if she had someone to walk with?

Germaine said she loved the springtime, working outside in her garden. She pointed out that she's been living this life for two years since Nat's initial diagnosis. She doesn't know what she'll do after Nathalie dies. When the focus has gone. I suggested she might then be good to herself. Germaine said she was going to take her time recovering. She said she knew the importance of facing the grief immediately, explaining that Nicole may not have gotten over their Mom's death because she didn't attend the funeral.

Will Nathalie's death help Nicole to grieve the loss of her mother?

Germaine and I talked in the Atrium for about an hour. It was so helpful for me. I am aware that I'm becoming more compassionate and understanding. We talked about Nathalie's funeral. Germaine was reflecting on whether or not to have the wig placed on Nathalie's head. Nathalie didn't like the wig, wearing it only to go out in public. Germaine said we've gotten used to Nathalie bald. We have. Nathalie loved hats so perhaps she'd look for Nathalie's favourite hat – a black velvet one – and she'd give it to the funeral director.

Chantal and Germaine spent some time last weekend talking about what clothing they would choose for Nathalie's body. Germaine hasn't been the kind of parent who goes into her children's rooms searching for 'stuff'. She's always respected their privacy. She hasn't gone into Nathalie's room since she went into hospital except to get her underwear and pyjamas.

Nothing else has been touched.

I talked with Germaine about cleaning out my mother's dresser and closet about a year after she died. It was so difficult seeing the tattered under clothing, some with pins in them. There was delicate lingerie and nighties still in pristine condition. Gifts of her favourite cologne and other lotions untouched. Did my mother, so generous to others, feel unworthy of receiving?

We talked about how love continues even after death, becoming stronger in the absence of the physical reality of the beloved person. We talked about what happens to a person once they've died and about our mutual belief that there is no hell. We believe hell is what we're going through right now. Hell is the suffering of the dying. It's the pain of watching someone you love slowly passing away. Germaine said she shouldn't say she doesn't believe in Hell as she's a Catholic. I encouraged her to say whatever she believed without slipping into shame or guilt.

I shared my belief that when someone dies they don't go up to heaven but rather they slip behind a veil we cannot see, that they are still with us. I told her of Jeannie asking me where I thought Mom was not too long after she'd died. I said she was in heaven. Daddy said she was an angel. I remember clearly not giving the words conscious thought but rather that they simply slipped out of my mouth without censor.

I often feel my mother and father's presence surrounding me with love and care. I find it healing and reassuring.

Isn't heaven a place filled with the fragrance of flowers, the singing of birds, the buzzing of bees and fluttering butterflies? Hummingbirds sup from the brilliant red blossoms of a trumpet vine. Frogs sing their off-key arias nestled on lily pads in water gardens filled with colourful fish. Water hyacinths float on the ponds' surfaces, their lavender blooms bathing the eye in beauty. Japanese Maples dance from the garden's every corner. Benches of every conceivable material invite one to spend time in prayer or meditation. One bench, in particular, made of stone is covered with Woolly Thyme so that when one sits the pungent scent penetrates every pore. Here there are no judgements. No one is in a hurry. People smile and greet each other with gentle warmth and love. No harsh words are spoken. No one's voice is raised in anger. The vulnerable are free from physical violence.

Returning from my reverie, I hope our conversation brought her comfort.

For the first time Germaine thanked me for our time together. I can feel how much spending time with me helps her. I'm not her sister so we don't carry baggage from our childhood. I listen to her with my full attention.

The Atrium is soothing and comforting. I could sit there for hours working on my studies. If I find I can't study once Nathalie's gone I could come here.

Germaine said Charlotte has offered to come and sit with Nathalie to give Germaine a break. Germaine doesn't want anyone sitting with Nathalie except family.

Though I've disagreed throughout that Nathalie hasn't been told she's dying, I can see that Germaine has thought through at some length each decision she's made. She doesn't want to make any mistakes! She has devoted herself to Nathalie with everything else taking second place. She's been like a mother lion protecting her cub against danger and harm. Absolutely fierce. Brooking no fools.

Germaine doesn't believe Nathalie will live to the weekend. Germaine has stopped praying Novenas asking that God heal Nathalie. The rosary is what Germaine now prays asking God to take Nathalie home, out of her suffering. Germaine wishes Nathalie would say something to her about dying.

Nathalie is known all over the 4th floor. I ran into a parishioner from our church last night who works at the hospital. As soon as I mentioned that Guy's niece was dying she immediately asked if that was the 'girl' who was given a graduation in the Atrium. When I said yes she said that everyone was so moved by this event that there wasn't a dry eye in the house.

Germaine hasn't smoked for a year. I didn't notice.

December 19, 1999
When Guy and I went to the hospital last night Nathalie had lots of company in her room including Marty, Chantal, Darrin and Rob.

Nathalie's sitting up in bed looking seconds away from dying surrounded by strong, healthy young people all older than her, including her pregnant sister. What must it have felt like to her knowing she's dying? She doesn't speak because of the sores on and in her mouth.

While we were there I did some questions on my final assignment of Horticulture II. I've come to the place where I have to input into the computer and begin to bring my answers to a close before I forward them on to the University of Guelph. I wonder how I'll do? I like getting high marks.

Guy did some work outside yesterday preparing for winter; mulching, draining hoses and putting them away as well as putting the Buddha and the green bench in the shed. He also put up the string of multi-coloured lights outside. He placed cedar roping across the gates between our house and our neighbours'. Today he'll put up the indoor lights in my room. Tomorrow he'll put them up in the kitchen.

I wonder what I'll do with this journal when Nathalie dies. Will I continue to record in it as Germaine goes through the grieving process? Will I get to the place where I feel I want to do something else with it? Write a novel? Short story? Poem? Essay? Novella? What will Germaine say when I tell her I've been writing about what's been happening? Will I learn more after Nathalie's gone as I walk through the grieving process with Germaine?

December 22, 1999

On Monday night, Guy went to the hospital alone. Last night we went together. I didn't go in the room. I couldn't bring myself to pretend anymore or to smile when I feel like crying. It's one of my regrets. I settled into the chair in the Atrium, placing my books on the table to study. I was just getting started when Germaine arrived. She stayed with me for two hours from 7 to 9 p.m.

Germaine began by telling me that Nathalie had nearly died – again – this morning. The doctor came in to see her and asked how long she'd been 'like that'. He meant the loud moaning. Germaine told him it had gone on for some time now. I'm not sure how long she meant but I believe Nat had been moaning in her sleep for a few days at least, perhaps longer. The sounds were becoming much louder, so loud that Germaine had to put on earphones in order to watch television. Even this didn't block out the sound. The doctor did something with Nathalie and things are quieter.

I spoke with Germaine about my undergoing six sessions of hypnotherapy. I told her about the past lives the work had uncovered. Germaine wondered aloud if we've lived before. She queried whether Nathalie's life was cut short because of something she'd done in a past one. Rhetorical questions. I know that Nathalie thought about these very things. This is what we talked about when we were together.

No IVs now. Just a needle given for pain. Nathalie's no longer drinking but simply having her mouth wiped out for her comfort. When she coughs she has to go inside her mouth and manually bring out the mucus or whatever it is. She's covered with bedsores on the parts of her body Germaine can see – her legs, feet and hands. There is no longer any cell rejuvenation. She hardly speaks at all and when she does she's confused as to time and place. She responds very slowly to a question, taking as much as five minutes.

During the weeks Nathalie has been in hospital Germaine and Nathalie have had several visits from a woman who does therapeutic touch. When the therapist touched the top of Germaine's head she began to sob, her feelings just a breath beneath the surface of her skin. I encouraged her to continue to have some kind of touch therapy once Nat is gone. We talked about the space which will be left for Germaine when Nat is dead and the importance of accepting the absence. This is easy to say when most of us do things to fill up the space. What will Germaine do? What will Gerry do?

What will I do?

Nathalie's friend, Sammi, was again on Germaine's mind. She went on and on about her and how much she couldn't stand her. I think Germaine feels pushed out of the way when it comes to Sammi because Nathalie is clear she still wants to see her. Sammi is Nathalie's best friend. This friend came to see Nat the other day after more than a week's absence. She broke down in the room sobbing so that Nat had to – once again – issue her warning, "No crying"!

Germaine wonders if Sammi will return to Nathalie's room.

4 North's unit manager has said that maybe Nat may go home for Christmas Eve day around 4 p.m., returning at 10. Nathalie wants (a) to go home for Christmas, and (b) to sleep in her own bed. Germaine was asked if she was sure she was up to it and would be okay with whatever might happen. Germaine said she was tired, putting her head down on the table, but I know she didn't say this to the unit manager. Germaine told her she felt okay about it. Chantal and Darrin will be home by 4 o'clock as will Martin and Gerry. Nathalie will get to have Christmas with her family and Rob. I told Germaine we didn't have to be there if Nat didn't want and I don't think she does. I think I'll simply not go since I've agreed to spend the day at Germaine's cleaning the house to get ready for Nathalie's arrival.

In fact, Germaine told me I was invited for Christmas but only if I helped with the cleaning. I'd forgotten about that.

Germaine is still sleeping in the little room on the Palliative Care ward.

The nurses have implied that Germaine is too protective of Nathalie. Or was it the doctors? I'm not sure but she spoke about it last night. I do know that she wants someone from the family with Nathalie at all times. She doesn't want her to die alone. The truth is that we do die alone no matter if we're in a room filled with people. No one but us does our dying. Germaine would agree with this self-evident statement but it would be patronizing to say it to her. Jeannie says that the worst part of the dying process is yet to come. She says it's harder once the person has died to be a support to the grieving partner, parent or family member.

Germaine believes that Nat has had at least two out-of-body or near-death experiences. One was when she repeated that she was dying. The other was when she said, "It's really crowded up there." She told Germaine she saw someone who looked like Germaine. Her maternal grandmother died in 1973 at the age of 57 and Germaine is her spitting image.

I believe in spite of talk to the contrary that Germaine isn't able to let Nathalie go – yet. This in spite of praying for God to take Nathalie and end her suffering. Germaine's heart isn't in it and she doesn't want her daughter to die. This makes sense to me! How can any mother, especially one as fierce as Germaine, ever want her child to die – no matter what the circumstances? She wants Nat's suffering to end but not for Nat to die! Even last night, with Nathalie clearly close to death Germaine spoke about Nathalie having to get strong again if she ever hoped to fully recover. It's amazing the mind's capacity to deny what's staring one right in the face.

Tonight we're not going to the hospital. We're going shopping and out for dinner. We'll go tomorrow night or Guy will. I'll need to do the laundry if I'm spending the day at Germaine's on Friday. I still want to spend a day baking cookies, date & nut and banana nut breads as well as some soup and chili.

PARADISE

May the angels bear you gently
To the loving arms of God.
May they lead you to a new day
Where the holy ones have trod.
May you dance with all the angels,
May you feast with all the saints.
May the God of all creation,
May the God of all the nations
Hold you gently to His face.

May the God of all creation
Hold you in His warm embrace.
May He welcome you as springtime
See the radiance of your face.
May you feast with all the angels
In this festival of love.
May He welcome you back home
To happiness and love.

May the holy ones before us
Lead you to the table there
Where there's food for all the people
No more sorrow, no more cares.
May you see the God who made us
Tender, loving, full of grace
May you know the deepest joy
Of dancing face to face.

December 23, 1999

This morning at 12:31 a.m. Nathalie died in her room. She was surrounded by her mother, father and brother.

It's amazing what can happen outside of your awareness.

Guy and I were asleep when the telephone rang. Guy answered. It was 1 a.m. It was Gerry.

Guy came back to bed but we couldn't sleep. I asked him if he wanted to go to the hospital about four times. He was afraid. I told him I'd call the hospital and speak to Gerry. I don't remember if Guy responded. I called and told Gerry we wanted to come to the hospital. There was just the slightest hesitation but then he said okay. Guy and I dressed as quickly as we could and were at the hospital before 2 a.m.

The cool air and quiet night were a contrast to our spirits.

My first image upon entering the room was of Germaine sitting beside the bed, stroking Nathalie's hands, arm and leg. We got hugs from everyone. The little room, once festooned, was now empty of Christmas celebration. The tiny body that housed the soul of our beloved girl was free of needles, IVs and oxygen mask. It looked lost in the hospital bed she'd rarely left for the past seven weeks.

There was a lovely basket filled with cookies, cheese, crackers, carrots and other snacks. Charlotte, kneeling by the bed saying the rosary, had brought them with her. Only Chantal and Darrin were absent. They'll arrive later today.

Rob was sitting quietly in a chair at the foot of Nathalie's bed.

It felt absolutely right to be there with everyone close to Nathalie.

We spent several hours in the room with Nathalie's body. Her spirit was gone. We spoke about her with laughter and tears. It was a precious and sacred time. I said something like, "The next person to come into the room to stay will wonder why there's such a wonderful feeling. Even the pores of the walls are filled with the energy of love which has gathered here over the past weeks."

I've never seen a dead body before without the benefit of

embalming. I've never spent time in the room of a dead person. It all felt so incredible in spite of the grief. There was an intimacy such as I've never experienced. It was like a cozy afghan, its weavings breathing comfort to our tired, sad bodies. Finally after weeks of holding back we were free to cry out our sorrow at our loss. To wonder at a God so greedy He couldn't leave her with us for just a moment longer.

A hospital chaplain was there. She was a strong, calm presence in the midst of the moment's incredulity. She told Guy and I how much it meant to Germaine that we'd offered her our support. She was the second person to tell us. Nelly, Guy's sister-in-law, was the first in her Christmas card.

Jeannie was right—you're not really prepared for death even when you know it's coming. I think we all thought she'd live until Christmas. Didn't we?

I have a sense of Rob's presence throughout this time in her room. He was sitting to my right. He was quiet. I don't think he spoke. I don't remember feeling any emotion coming from him but my sense is of a young man at peace. I wish I knew what he was feeling. I may never know.

I worried that Germaine might not be able to leave the room but she was the one to say, "It's time now". Guy and I, Rob and his mom left the room along with the chaplain. Germaine, Gerry and Martin stayed so they could say goodbye. When Germaine came out of the room for the last time she hugged the nurses. One of the lovely ones invited her to come back when she felt ready.

I hugged Germaine for a long time before leaving 4 North for good. I felt her legs give way so I held on tighter. I went with Germaine and Gerry to their home around 4 a.m. I offered her my arm so she could lean on me. She was exhausted. Outside the air was cold and crisp. The night sky was black and somewhere hidden behind the clouds a star shone.

Marty turned on the Christmas lights the minute we walked into the house. Rob and his mom arrived, having brought Germaine's car home for her so she wouldn't have to drive. Guy and Marty had cleaned up everything from the two rooms, Nathalie's and Germaine's. Guy told me he had checked to make sure they had everything. Then he covered Nathalie's body with the white coverlet before kissing her on the forehead in farewell. Guy thanked me for calling Gerry and for going to the hospital. He said he felt too uncertain and afraid. It felt good to have him thank me. We feel so close to each other. I'm glad he's decided not to go to Quebec City until after the funeral. It means he'll be with us for Christmas after all.

Rob's mom has offered to help clean the house if we're still going to do that. I'll have to check with Germaine. I don't feel right just going over without first talking with her. She knows what she wants and doesn't want. I want to respect that.

Germaine gave the little angel with the green wreath to Rob and asked him if he wanted to be noted in the obituary as Nathalie's special friend. I believe he was quite surprised. He simply nodded.

December 24, 1999

I pushed through my fear and called Germaine to see if we could come over before they were leaving for the funeral home. I took the sweater, vest and hat with me that I'd felt compelled to offer Germaine for Nathalie's body. I'd made the set years ago and never knew who was meant to own it.

Germaine was sitting on Nathalie's bed going through pictures for the funeral home as well as trying to sort out an outfit for her body. She was exhausted. Gerry kept coming into the room to show her another picture. Why do men always feel they have to DO something? Their need for action is often annoying to women. We want to work things out ourselves. We do this by talking things out with each other. We don't want the other person to give us advice or do 'it' for us. We're very capable of 'doing' whatever needs doing ourselves.

Once Guy and I were in the room, Guy hung the sweater ensemble on the door of Nathalie's closet. I showed Germaine the outfit. It didn't take her long to say she would not be using my offering as she hadn't seen Nathalie in it. In other words it didn't belong to Nat. After much consideration she chose a layered look in blacks, including the velvet hat Nathalie adored. Germaine wondered about the fact that everything was black but remembered that Nathalie loved wearing black. In fact black was her favourite 'colour'. Rob had said at one point that he felt her favourite colour was blue.

When Guy and I offered to go to the funeral home with them, Germaine was very open and glad to accept our offer. We made it clear we wouldn't go into the room with them but would stay outside just in case they needed our help with anything. However, Gerry was very vocal about telling us not to come. Martin, Chantal and Darrin would be there with them, he said. In fact Marty didn't go at all and Chantal and Darrin wrote the obituary before going to the funeral home with it. They appeared to have no intention of staying until we made it clear we were leaving.

When we left the funeral home we drove to the 'Tangled Garden'. I'd looked in the yellow pages earlier and liked the name. The florist's shop was very small but it was filled with lovely things for Christmas. We took our time looking as thoroughly as we could in a shop where you can take hours looking at all the items. After careful consideration we chose a round black container symbolizing the circle of life and death. The container had a Japanese feel to it which I loved. Guy chose a little angel. Two votive candles, one green one red typified the Christmas season Nathalie loved so much. One will be lit at all times when we're at the funeral home. Joseph, the floral designer, suggested green Bells of Ireland, so unusual at any time of the year. When they are left on their own they dry to a soft beige and must be handled with care for the petals will disintegrate if the hand is rough. At my request Joseph will surround the Bells with white pine for their fragrance, curly twig for definition and architectural structure. I felt confident to leave the remaining choices up to him. Perhaps hot pink Gerbera daisies so rich and flamboyant, a sharp contrast to the daintier Bells of Ireland? Maybe the strength of Protea, a flower native to South Africa? However the arrangement ends up looking I think it will be different.

Marty says he was told by Nathalie he couldn't cry until after the funeral. And he's keeping his promise. I do wish he wouldn't. He says his back is so sore he thinks it might break. I wonder what or who will break as a result of Nathalie's death. I wonder when Nat told him he couldn't cry until after the funeral?

This means she did talk to Marty about dying!!

Charlotte, Guy and I cleaned Germaine's house last night. Rob's mom cleaned the kitchen really thoroughly though Guy insisted on washing the floor. Rob's Mom also brought all kinds of food and goodies, some baked or prepared by her daughter including baklava, truffles, cookies of every shape and size. She said Germaine's freezer was packed with food as well as the fridge upstairs and the freezer on the lower level. There would be no need for me to bring any food!

I cleaned the upstairs and downstairs bathrooms while Guy scrubbed the floors. Guy also swept through the house. I dusted the living room – a little. I watered the Hibiscus. I hope it survives. It desperately needs more light. The rest of the plants looked watered.

Germaine seems much more settled, stronger even, since completing the funeral arrangements. She's spent a lot of time on the telephone talking long distance. The majority of her family lives out-of-town. She did cry while talking to Rob's mom and I.

Throughout this entire process I've not stopped thinking about Lynda, my own daughter. I wish she could create the floral tributes for the funeral. How beautiful they would be. How proud I'd be of her artistic ability. She used to tease me about mine saying I didn't like negative space, whereas she was not only comfortable with it but accentuated it in her flower arrangements. Lynda creates designs which are called 'high style' in the floral business. She loves flowers outside of the norm.

Nathalie would have approved.

How different Lynda's and my relationship from that enjoyed by Nathalie and Germaine. Not that their relationship was without problems. Nathalie sometimes felt smothered by

Germaine's overprotectiveness. But she also felt safe and secure in the shelter of her mother's profound love. It was always her mother she turned to meet her needs and wants. It was her mother to whom her head was turned in death.

Rob, Marty and Darrin will be three of the six pallbearers for Nathalie. Germaine will also ask three cousins. Claude and Pierrette will be here on Monday around 2 p.m. This is when the visitation will begin at the funeral home. Claude's wife, Nelly, will not travel in the winter because of the accident they were in a few years ago. I don't remember hearing about this. I must ask. Robert and Huguette came after all. They live in Montreal. Initially Huguette felt she couldn't leave her mother who suffers from Alzheimer's.

Guy's favourite aunt and uncle will not be here as they are not well. However, members of Gerry's family from out-of-town will be here including a brother and his children. Nathalie's godmother will also be coming. Germaine laughed and said how wise Nathalie was dying before Christmas to get Gerry's family to come to her funeral at Christmas time.

Guy and I aren't planning to go to Germaine's again until Sunday. We might not see them until Monday. Guy wasn't sure whether or not Germaine heard him when he said this as she was on the telephone and Gerry was watching television alone in the family room. Darrin's mom had gone shopping earlier in the day for food and brought tons of it over to the house.

Guy is going to change his departure for Quebec City from Sunday morning to the following Wednesday. I'm praying he'll be able to do so as I want him home with me until after the funeral. I know I'll then be able to let him go without complaint, albeit with sadness. He has Nathalie's obituary with him. It was in this morning's paper along with her high school graduation picture.

Guy and I are closer than we've ever been. Telling each other how much we love each other and sharing our thoughts and feelings. I'm a little more sensitive to Guy's needing to be involved in the decisions we make.

My article about Art Roth's garden at St. Clare Roman

Catholic School isn't in the paper after all. I am so disappointed. I don't know what happened but I'm calling the master gardener in charge of the column to see if she knows. My guess is the newspaper won't even publish it if they didn't today.

Nathalie's death has already taught me the importance of enjoying life or 'seizing the day', as the little plastic card says on top of my two drawer file cabinet. The importance of laughing and crying and of being myself whether or not people like me. Not trying to live up to what I think other people want and being true to myself.

This is difficult.

December 25, 1999

Guy has been successful in changing his leaving for Quebec until 6 a.m. on Wednesday, December 29th. I'm so glad. He'll be gone just ten days returning January 7th, 2000 at 8:30 p.m. Not that I'm counting!

Guy talked to Germaine on the phone last evening before we went to ten o'clock mass. Nathalie gave her a birthstone ring for Christmas. Rob gave Nathalie the gift of a star. A star is sparkling in the heavens with Nathalie's name pinned to it.

I gave Guy a stargazer I purchased from Lee Valley Tools in Ottawa.

Nathalie gave Rob a ring with 'Thank You' engraved inside. Germaine and Gerry gave Rob a gold pen also inscribed with 'Thank You'.

Why did I fret this whole time about her not knowing she was dying? She knew. She was all prepared. I wonder if someone helped her? Sammi? Marty?

Christmas Eve Debbie, Guy and I went to ten o'clock mass. It was lovely and it was over by 11:15 p.m. Much shorter than when our former priest was with us but not as beautiful. Our new priest rationalized that it was simpler and therefore more appropriate for this solemn and sacred time of the year. I'm not sure I agree. This man is more traditional which I don't think I care for. But then again it must appeal to some part of my nature since it brings with it a structure and security I seem to need. Now and then he gives me a lovely smile.

The church was decorated with two small conifers covered in tiny lights. The altar was embraced by dozens of red and cream-coloured poinsettias. A creche graced the front of the altar. The processional was led by the priest carrying the baby Jesus whom he placed in the manger. The homily was given with passion.

Five parcels arrived yesterday from Honolulu for Greg in care of me. He had told me on the phone that they were gifts for all of us in Windsor. I'm curious what's inside ALL of them. They're different weights.

Greg and Janina will be here tomorrow around 2 p.m. He'll take his time driving as there's lots of snow around London. There's none here. The day is chilly but it's sunny and bright.

Guy wants to go to Germaine's today. My thought is to give them some time as a family. They'll be inundated with people beginning on Monday for at least two days. They'll need us more in the days, weeks and months ahead when no one else is around and they are feeling the pain of their loss.

I asked Guy if he'd like to be a Hospice volunteer? He said he'd like to just sit with a dying person. He doesn't feel he can talk to them about their feelings. Wouldn't it be good if we could be a volunteer couple? He could do the sitting and I could do the working with feelings, listening, etc. We'll see how things play out in the new year.

Germaine's worried about where the out-of-town people will go between visitations on Monday. She wants them to come to her house to eat the burden of food that's accumulated. I still don't know if I'm going in the afternoon but some food needs to be cooked so someone needs to be in charge. Her next door neighbour? Me? She said she trusts us both!

I didn't offer.

I told her that for the first time in her life, perhaps, she would need all her strength just to get through the next few days. She would have to leave all the practical matters to others.

She agreed. It is a very unfamiliar position for the sister who loves family to visit and to have to cook for all of them.

How I enjoyed the huge dinner after Christmas Eve's midnight mass.

I'm hoping my sons will go to the funeral or the funeral home. Debbie said last night that Blake plans to go but she's not sure if she will be able to go. Later she said she was going to ask her sister to babysit for her so she could go too.

The Galileo thermometer is really lovely. I bought it for Guy for Christmas. But in truth I bought it for myself.

I'm really aware tonight that this whole process with Nathalie is also about Lynda's estrangement from me/us. I vacillate between feeling really sad and really angry, wondering what could have been done differently.

Perhaps nothing?

We're going to Blake and Debbie's around 4 p.m. staying for dinner and the evening. We'll play a game, perhaps 'Chicken Soup for the Soul'? My annual family game! How ironic.

December 30, 1999

So much to write I don't know where to start. We had a good time at Blake's on Christmas Day. Why don't we go more often? I made the gravy. I brought mints and cookies. They gave us an 8 x 10 framed picture of 'The Bruiser' aka Brandon Christopher Iain for our Christmas gift. We played 'Chicken Soup for the Soul' and Debbie's answers to the questions were very revealing, thought provoking and surprising. They showed a depth I haven't given her credit for and a spirituality I didn't realize was there. I knew she was religious.

When Blake was asked a question about when he learned the true meaning of love his face was filled with pain. I could feel the tears well up in me at his simple answer. We do need to know that we're worthy of unconditional love. If we don't believe it or haven't experienced it from someone even for a moment then how can we receive it when it's offered? We need to know we're worthy just because we have been given the gift of life and for no other reason. Not because we're smart, or beautiful, or rich, or have a wonderful job. We need to know we are loved so we in turn will be able to love. Every hair on our head is numbered the Bible says. This kind of love is mysterious, unfathomable, our language too inadequate to attempt even to express. We are known so well and held in the palm of His hand. No matter what happens to us, around us, by us, this love never wavers or fails. I have come to know in my heart the truth of this love.

I believe Nathalie knew this and wanted us to know it too. She knew that we don't have much time to truly enjoy life. We are meant to live passionately and immediately. We mustn't wait. This is no dress rehearsal, someone said. This is IT. The play's on stage. Now.

On December 26th Guy helped get the spare room ready for Janina and Greg, who arrived from Toronto around 1:15 p.m. Guy and I left them for about two hours to go to Germaine's to set up the tables and chairs for the supper on Monday, the 27th. I made a chicken dinner with lots of vegetables for supper. We enjoyed ourselves for the remainder of the day and evening. Greg had brought us such a lovely basket filled with goodies from Honolulu. My basket was filled with French Lavender incense, lavender essential oil, a lavender aromatherapy candle, lavender mineral bath salts, herbal tea 'Calm' as well as a CD 'Yoga Meditation'. Guy's basket had the same herbal tea, peach fruit spread, passion fruit syrup, macadamia nut butter, a lovely crunch, nutty candy (guess who ate that?) and dried fruits. Greg's sweater and pants fit him perfectly and Janina loved her purses, especially the little raspberry coloured one. She didn't wear the watch except briefly.

Monday, December 27th I decided I wouldn't come home between visitations after all. I wanted to go to Germaine's with Guy. I gave Greg $ 20.00 toward Chinese food and he and Janina spent about three hours with Blake and Debbie.

Greg drove me to Sears in the morning and I found a soft green sweater with figures on it to go with my oatmeal coloured pants for today's visitation; casual but chic. I wore my Birkenstocks or I wouldn't have been able to even stand up for more than a minute or two. Tomorrow I'll wear my boots to go to the cemetery. I also found a lovely suit. Unfortunately it was too big. A stone blue cardigan caught my eye so I purchased it. I'll wear it tomorrow with my black pants and white blouse with the large, flat collar. I feel good about what I have to wear. At least I won't look completely out of place although in comparison with some others I'll be underdressed.

We arrived at the funeral home around 1:20 p.m. Germaine, Gerry, Marty, Chantal, Darrin and Rob were the only ones there. The public wouldn't arrive until 2 p.m.

The huge room was already banked with floral arrangements including the one Guy and I sent. Our unique arrangement typified Nathalie. It consisted of three Bells of Ireland at the back facing each other looking down over the rest of the arrangement. Joseph had placed a Protea beside the angel Guy had chosen. Two rich rosy pink Gerberas were sunk deep into the arrangement for depth. There were blue/black berry branches and cedar boughs along with a striking green luminescent grass. The arrangement's difference and beauty made it stand out from the rest of the floral gifts. Germaine couldn't seem to take her eyes off of it.

However, the florist had forgotten the votive candles so someone called and they brought them over immediately with profuse apologies. The candle was lit and remained lit throughout the rest of the day and night until I blew it out at 9 p.m.

Nathalie's body was dressed in familiar clothing. A flocked blue top and velvet jacket had replaced the initial choice to wear black. Her black velvet hat was resting in the upper left corner of the casket. The casket was a spectacular metallic blue with silver handles and other relief. It had a soft blue lining. Nathalie's body looked so different from the tiny shell lying on the hospital bed, the effect of the embalming and the street clothes making nearly a shocking difference. As I looked down into her face I remembered the poignancy of the hospital vigil.

The starkness of death—its cold finality were evident in the hospital room. It was true, in other words. At the funeral home I kept expecting Nathalie to sit up or to see her chest move. The addition of the make-up and clothes made her seem more alive than dead. The reality in the hospital with the love and intimacy in room 4102 far outstripped this pretty exterior. There was instead a sense of removal. A sense of unreality.

There were flowers from Essex Engine Pipefitters. Many friends I didn't know. Rob's family, Rob – a dozen roses sitting just above and behind the casket near Nathalie's head. A red rose casket spray from the family and Rob, ordered by Darrin I believe, which included some winter greenery and berries. A few of the latter I have in my red jacket pocket. There was a statuesque Peace Lily clothed in a white ribbon and gold foil. A fragrant White Lily was in full dress. Rob's mom gave a country basket. A beautiful burnished basket filled with plants, including an Azalea covered in white and pink blooms from Darrin's cousin.

There were prayer cards with Nathalie's picture.

Darrin, Chantal and Darrin's mom had created a collage of pictures of Nathalie taken throughout her life. In the centre was her graduation picture from high school. The collage was placed on an easel about halfway along the far outside wall. It became a gathering place for family and friends throughout the vigil.

It was the first funeral I've been to where the median age was about 25. I've never seen so many young people at a funeral. There were 94 people in the afternoon and they didn't stop coming in the evening. The room was so packed for the evening prayers that it felt hot in spite of the bitter weather. There were 300 people total.

Some people's faces come to mind as I sit and recall the events of the past few days. Kate's face in the congregation at the funeral mass at St. Anne's Church in Tecumseh. A warm and friendly face amongst the throng of people who filled the church for the funeral mass on a cold winter's day. Rob's mom who came to Germaine's and cleaned the kitchen, brought tons of food, visited Nathalie in the hospital countless times, spent every moment at the funeral home visitation and again the day of the funeral right up until the very end. Herself the mother of five children.

Jennifer, Nathalie's friend, who flew in from Calgary just for the funeral. Short, dark hair adorned with the little clips so fashionable today in a cranberry coloured blouse and black skirt. My first sight of her was at the funeral home on Monday. She was standing just inside the doorway of the room and sobbing as if her heart was breaking. I simply beheld her for a few moments then I knew I must offer her some solace, some frame for her sorrow, so I opened my arms and she slipped into them like fingers putting on a familiar glove. I hugged her very tightly for a while before asking her name. "Jennifer," she said.

"I've got a granddaughter about your age named Jennifer," I said.

I invited her to look at the collage first before she approached the casket, but she told me she already had. She said she was there with friends but she wasn't ready yet. I asked her when was the last time she'd seen Nathalie. "One and one-half years ago," she said.

I said, "Nat will seem greatly changed to you. She's bald now, which is how we remember her. This will be difficult for you." We talked together for a few more minutes before I released her to walk over once more to the gathering at the collage. I saw her sobbing in Germaine's arms in front of Nathalie's casket just moments later. She came to the funeral home, funeral and Knights of Columbus Hall for the luncheon following the burial service.

She approached me again and said, "Thank you".

"Thank YOU," I said.

"You're welcome," she responded.

I'll never forget the image of her grief and her willingness to accept my offer of comfort with such ease.

I remember Germaine and her fierceness on behalf of her daughter. Her determination to get things right including the manner in which Nathalie's body was dressed in the casket.

Her inner strength and her vulnerability and sorrow. Her absolute focus on Nathalie's recovery during these past two years and especially the last two months caring for Nathalie to the very best of her ability without concern or without seeming concern as to what others thought of her or if she might be offending anyone with her behaviour and actions. Her absolute devotion, spending many nights in the hospital on a makeshift bed in Nathalie's room. Only later would she be given a separate bedroom in the Palliative Care unit on the same floor where she had a sofa bed, two chairs and a television.

She continued to function and do what was necessary. She looked lovely at the funeral home and mass. She was standing at the burial site without any boots on in her high heels. No hat. It was 20 degrees below zero with blowing snow and high winds. The first blizzard of the winter of 1999/2000. Her increasing awareness in the face of continued shock and denial about what was happening to her daughter. Never believing, truly, that Nathalie would die yet preparing for death's inevitability. A true contradiction. A paradox. My love for her deepened as each day went by even when I disagreed with her or felt left out or under appreciated. Always my love came through and won out over my negativity.

I understand at some level the terrible hole Nathalie's death will leave in Germaine's life. A hole which will not – cannot – ever be filled. I can hear Germaine saying softly to me early in the afternoon on Monday as we were waiting for the rest of our family to arrive from out of town that she was afraid she would break down when Claude came. When he arrived I saw her weeping in his arms. She said she didn't know what it was about seeing him that caused this reaction. Only that she knew for certain it would. I can hear her asking me if she could take 'our' arrangement home.

I remember knowing that this process isn't over yet. Knowing I would be privileged to go through the grieving with her, too. Knowing that though there were many wonderful people present for the funeral including both extended family and friends of each family member, it would be Guy and I who would walk with Germaine and Gerry as they continued on their own journey without Nathalie. I remember reminding myself of this truth whenever I felt left out. The thought sustained and fed me knowing how blessed I was and how blessed I would continue to be no matter what happened in the future.

Germaine: A Class Act

Gerry: Jeannie said a father may never forgive himself for not saving his daughter from death. It makes no rational sense, of course, but then so much in life doesn't, does it? Gerry at the hospital for ever-increasing periods of time, sometimes overnight. Gerry looking for and finding hopeful signs of recovery. Some miracle which would save his daughter's life. Gerry saying to me at the funeral home how much as a parent you want to be rid of the child because of the things they do to you – thoughtless, hurtful things. How you just wish they'd go away and how now you'd give anything in the world to have them back. It was Gerry who called at 1 a.m. on December 23rd to tell us Nathalie was dead. It was Gerry I called at the hospital to see if we might come to be with them. It was Gerry who bought me a cup of tea and a cookie one night at the hospital cafeteria. It was Gerry who spent thousands of dollars for his daughter's funeral, burial and marker. Gerry who talked at length with me one night early in November. He talked about his love of fishing and camping. Gerry who's daughter was buried at St. Anne's Cemetery in Tecumseh. Gerry a father who won't leave now. His legacy is here. His name will be engraved on the grave's marker alongside his wife's and daughter's. No matter how much he longs for a different life away from this city, the simple truth remains: he will not leave his daughter's grave. This would constitute desertion.

Martin 'Marty': older brother spending time at the hospital with Nathalie. Marty talking to her in a way only he could. Making jokes – filling the air with his youthful music and optimism. Marty not crying when Nathalie died because she told him 'don't' cry' until after the funeral. He didn't succeed –

thank God – but oh how hard he tried. Marty who had lots of friends come to the funeral home out of respect for him. He seems to be a very popular guy. Marty so tall and handsome. Martin one of the pallbearers for his sister's casket.

Back to Monday, December 27th

We waited for the rest of our family to arrive and began to worry when it passed two o'clock with no sign of them. I don't remember who arrived first but we were very happy to finally see them.

Just as Germaine had predicted, when Claude came to her she fell into his arms.

Gerry's side of the family arrived including his brother and family as well as Nathalie's godmother. Gerry's face lit up when he saw his family. He was so delighted they'd come. It's sad that we don't bring joy to our family while they're still alive or in happy times.

I remember Germaine saying that Nathalie knew what she was doing, dying before Christmas ensuring that Gerry's family would attend her funeral. Unfortunately since I don't speak French I had little to do with them except to say 'Bonjour' from time to time. I do regret not learning to speak French though not enough to attempt to learn it now. I would at least like to say Germain (Gerry) and Germaine's names correctly!

One woman at the funeral visitation stood out. She had suffered from breast cancer and Nathalie had brought her a beautiful bouquet of flowers while this woman was in hospital. She and her husband were there throughout the entire visitation period. I'd see them often. They were visibly weeping.

Many of the family went to Germaine's for supper after the 2 to 5 p.m. visitation. A meal had been prepared by Germaine's next door neighbours. There was lasagna, including a vegetarian one for Rob, coleslaw, salad, French bread and a sort of pasta soup sans bowls. Pat had prepared the entire meal. Dennis had helped in bringing it over. They were at the evening visitation and again at the funeral. Darrin's

Grandmother, newly engaged to her soon-to-be third husband, brought wonderful pastries. There were cold cuts and cheese. I sat beside Rob with Chantal, Darrin and Guy who kept flitting about like a pouter pigeon. Germaine, Micheline, Pierrette and Nicole – the four sisters – sat at the next table with their sister-in-law, Huguette. The rest were in the basement.

Prayers were held at the funeral home at 8 p.m. A man from St. Anne's R. C. Church led. I don't remember what he said. I don't even know how pertinent it was to Nathalie's life. The room was jammed with people sitting on the sofas and chairs as well as standing along the walls. It was very warm, unlike the afternoon's coolness.

I tried to take pictures of the floral arrangements and the collage but our camera wasn't working. When I took it to Black's Camera later to have it looked at the film hadn't been put in tightly enough. The camera was fine. It's clear to me in hindsight that I wasn't meant to take any pictures. I was meant to create a picture with words.

I don't recall if I ever saw Rob cry. I think he found it very difficult to be there but I'm not sure why. Nothing to do? He didn't feel as sad as many people may have thought? Did Germaine's warmth and affection sustain him? Charlotte told me that going through this with Rob brought them closer together and how grateful she was for that.

The funeral home ran out of prayer cards at the end of the two days. When I returned to the funeral home to get the basket I'd chosen, with Germaine's permission, I didn't think not to go into 'Nat's' room. It was already occupied by another person's body. The casket flanked with dozens of floral tributes. I thought to myself, how quickly the room had changed—occupied as it was now with another's person remains. It didn't feel right. Too quick? What if the walls could talk? What would they say? The funeral director ushered me rather quickly into a side room where the flowers were now on movable stands waiting to be picked up by whomever would arrive to take them away.

Friday, December 31, 1999

Tuesday morning woke to the winter's first blizzard. Blowing snow, bone-chilling winds with little visibility made travelling E. C. Row to the funeral home before 9 a.m. treacherous. Today would be our final moments with Nat's body.

I wonder where she is?

I became concerned for all the out-of-town visitors, especially Greg and Janina. I asked him later if he'd consider staying overnight but he said he couldn't. He'd used up all his time and had to go to work the next day or he wouldn't be paid. I felt sad to see the look of panic in his eyes.

When we arrived there were already people at the funeral home. We stood around talking quietly going up to look into the casket, hoping to absorb through osmosis the face of our dear Nathalie. The extended family were invited to 'say their last goodbyes' as 10 a.m. closed in; the time of departure for St. Anne's Church just down the road.

As we were leaving Blake and Debbie came in but we had just a moment before we had to leave for our cars. We were the ninth car from the beginning which included two white limousines at the front of the procession. If anything, it felt colder than earlier. The sky was pregnant with snow. Claude was going to Canadian Tire to find winter tires for his son's car. Did he manage to find some?

While we waited in our van for the procession to begin we saw the pallbearers carry Nat's casket to the back of the limousine. Germaine and Gerry entered the other car. Slowly each car slid forward behind each other like dozens of piggyback trailers. The funeral director was directing traffic on Tecumseh Road. He looked frozen in place with only his arms moving. His head was bare. As we moved along Tecumseh Road cars stopped to make way. Only seven cars were able to park in front of the church so we drove around to the back parking lot lining up once again bumper to bumper in preparation for the final short drive to the burial ground at St. Anne's Cemetery.

As we exited our cars the winter wind licked our faces like

the rough tongue of a tiger's cub. We fought with the cold catching our breath each time with a gasp. Guy wondered aloud if we should wait for the family but I wanted to go inside the church to find my son and granddaughter. Greg and Janina would be waiting for us.

Heedless of Guy's wishes I went into the church, which appeared to be empty. Then I saw Greg and Janina sitting close to the front of the church on the far right hand side. I went to them immediately.

As the church began to fill up I didn't notice that Guy wasn't with me. By then Blake and Debbie were seated to my left. I still don't know exactly when Guy came to sit at the end of the pew beside Blake. I wanted him to sit beside me but he brushed me off indicating that he planned to stay right where he was on the aisle.

Soon the pallbearers entered the church. They walked slowly down the aisle carrying the precious cargo on their young shoulders. The rest of the family followed with Rob sitting in the second row of the church on the right side a few rows in front of us. By this time the church was filled with people.

It was very cold.

St. Anne's Church was beautiful, filled with statues decorated in gold leaf. Two tall majestic Christmas trees covered with twinkling clear lights as well as many poinsettias, cedar garlands and other decorations honouring the time of year enlivened the altar.

Where are you Nat? Are you loving every moment? Is the church too cold for your warm spirit?

The priest invited the family to cover Nathalie's casket with a large white cloth symbolizing her baptism. Fr. Larry Brunet, St. Anne's parish priest, began to speak alternating between French and English, a reflection of the congregation's bilingualism. Patrick, Nathalie's first cousin, read the first reading in English. Her French cousin read the second reading in French. Her cousin's wife read the Prayers of the Faithful in French and English.

I don't remember Father's words but they were said with caring and compassion recognizing the pain of losing a child/woman as young as Nathalie.

The music was beautiful. My favourite songs. On Eagle's Wings. Be Not Afraid. Debbie whispered that these were the songs she wanted at her funeral. I told her, "Me too". She said she'd sing them at my funeral.

The coup de grace of the day was the piper who mourned Nathalie's body into and out of the church. The sound of the pipes sent chills down my spine. I watched Blake's face as the music from his Celtic ancestors rang throughout the womb of the church. Quietly, Blake said, "No dissing the pipes, Mom!" I hadn't said a word, wanting only to see if they moved him. They did.

Later at the burial the piper played 'Amazing Grace' in the midst of the snow and cold. Was that the angels I heard singing? Were they welcoming Nathalie into Paradise even as we stood guard over her casket? When the music ended it was so quiet I could even hear the whispers of protest from the snow under our feet.

After the service as I hurried down the aisle to go to the van, there to my left near the back of the church was Kate. I reached out to her hugging and thanking her for coming. I was hoping she'd be at the burial.

Throughout the funeral mass Guy was openly crying or struggling for composure. Blake reached out to him in the awkward way men comfort one another. The love obvious in the gentle gesture.

Later as Guy and I stood outside on the church's front steps Guy moved as if to go to the limousine but then stopped himself. I'm struggling to get him to come to the van with me. He wore neither hat nor boots. He told me he could see Nathalie's sweet face smiling up at him as they exchanged their nightly ritual of rubbing the tops of each other's bald heads.

He was haunted.

My dear darling man, so filled with love, so unable to express it.

The casket was placed in the first limousine for its final trip to the cemetery.

The priest in a black velvet hat pulled down to protect his vulnerable ears invited everyone to huddle closer. The casket nestled in the snow was covered in roses. A number of floral tributes were already beginning to succumb to the frigid air. Martine, Guy's niece and his sister-in-law Huguette were to my left, Guy to my right. Blake and Debbie were farther over in my direct line of vision but at the end of the group to the left. There had to be at least 75 people present. More than I've ever seen at the site of a burial. The Calgary Jennifer stood directly opposite looking into my eyes from time to time.

I worried about Guy still with no hat or boots hoping the crush of bodies would keep away any potential illness. I wanted to protect him forever from sickness and death; to hold him beside me safe from harm. Father spoke with continued care and concern before the piper's lament rang out. It soared to the heavens. Blake was sobbing.

Amazing Grace, how sweet the sound
That saved a wretch like me
I once was lost but now am found
Was blind but now I see.

The song cannot be sung without moving me to tears. My own life is a testament to its truth. My heart filled both with gratitude and wonder at God's forgiveness to the humans who daily break His heart.

Slowly, one by one, each of us kissed the palm of our hand placing it on the casket. Gerry reached forward and gave a rose to family and friends – one by one. I gave mine to Pat, Germaine's neighbour. The lady who cooked the Monday meal and cabbage rolls for Germaine when she needed them the most.

She whispered that she felt the roses should go to family members.

We moved toward our cars reluctant to leave behind the

once beautiful girl. I prayed her body would be safe inside the box lined with silken blue. I knew her spirit soared and danced above the pain she'd endured on earth.

We had a perfectly terrible lunch in a cold, sterile room at the Knights of Columbus Hall. I wanted to go back to Germaine's and be with my family there in the cozy familiarity of her home. Instead Guy and I sat with people who wished they were elsewhere. I felt alone and out of place in much the same way I'd felt when first meeting this family. I realized that I could have learned French at some point during the past 25 years and maybe the sense of isolation wouldn't have been so great. I would have been able to speak with my family and, in turn, with their Quebec family.

Jennifer came to thank me again before she left the luncheon. She was returning home to Calgary the next day.

January 1, 2000

When I was writing to Dixie, one of my garden pals, yesterday I came upon the theme of the book I'll write. It will be about what happened in Nathalie's room after she died. We were all together laughing, crying, talking, being still. Jeannie said the room was filled with angels. It was the most magnificent moment of my life. Better even than what I'd experienced when I was received into the church at Easter time in 1995. And that time was extraordinary. I knew with certainty that (a) there is life after death, (b) Nathalie's once vibrant body was now a shell. The spirit that had animated the body had gone to places unknown except to God (c) we're here to learn life lessons to deepen our spiritual growth (d) we're here to love and care about one another. 'To be Christ to one another,' Jeannie would say. I wonder who said it first? (e) we're here to help people less fortunate than we are and (f) God exists. He/She/It is pure, unbounded love.

He is also a greedy God. 'He will not rest until we rest in Him' it says somewhere in the Bible.

This mystery can be difficult to grasp and claim in the face of Nathalie's suffering and the grief her family will bear for the rest of their lives. In the midst of life we are in death. Who said that? Life is a paradox; two apparently completely opposite truths coexisting. But not simply parallel, inseparable. Two sides of the same coin? Alpha and Omega – the beginning and the end. There is no opening. No doors or windows. If they are divided and I say – if – it's by a veil of gossamer so thin that except for a very few mortals we can't see it or see through it. These two entities, if that's the correct word – and I'm not sure there is a correct word, flow back and forth and through each other. Yet here too the paradox exists. They are separate too.

"The spirit of the Sovereign Lord is upon me, because the Lord has appointed me to bring good news to the poor. He has sent me to comfort the brokenhearted and to announce that captives will be released and prisoners will be freed. He has sent me to tell those who mourn that the time of the Lord's favor has come and with it, the day of God's anger against their enemies. To all who mourn in Israel, he will give beauty for ashes, joy instead of mourning, praise instead of despair. For the Lord has planted them like strong and graceful oaks for his own glory."
Isaiah 61: 1 – 3

I'm alone on this the first day of the year 2000. This is, however, not the first year of the new century. That's not until next year. I have prayed that someone will invite me to spend some time today with them but then endeavoured to leave it with God. I am thinking a great deal about Rob and Charlotte. I would like to call them to see if they would be willing to talk with me about what happened for them throughout the process of Nathalie's dying and death. More specifically I would like to know what happened for them in Nathalie's room after she died.

Pierrette is doing volunteer work to raise awareness for the need for unrelated bone marrow donors. I don't remember Germaine ever speaking about whether or not the possibility of related bone marrow donors was explored. It seems in many ways an unlikely work. Usually a match can't be found, I thought.

In Toronto some years ago a little Chinese girl was dying and her family went public looking for persons of Asian descent to come forward and be tested. It cost $ 75.00 for each test. No matches were ever found from literally hundreds of willing donors.

The little girl died.

I feel as if this time I have alone is meant to show me the truth about being human. We ARE alone in the physical sense. Each of us can only truly experience anything through our individual senses. Empathy is a fleeting thing at best when it works – if it works. A faith in God – a God of love – is an absolute necessity to keep from falling into the abyss. Someone said that religion is an opiate for the masses. I don't remember whom. But for me a faith in God – not religion – is an absolutely vital part of my willingness to go on living. I get frightened sometimes when I think of what I would do without it. Life is too difficult – too painful – too uncertain – too random. The only thing that makes any sense at all is a faith in a Power greater than myself.

Years ago I bought a sculpture created by an artist from Northern Ontario. It had been fashioned from the burl of a tree. On the stand that held the piece was a plaque with the words, "All else is vanity".

The most difficult thing is to keep my heart open in the midst of my sorrow.

Jeannie said perhaps I didn't touch Nathalie's body because I KNEW it wasn't Nathalie. That would be nice to think but I'm not sure I thought that at all at the time. I just don't like the feeling of cold flesh. Jeannie also asked me if I wouldn't have had anything further to do upon leaving Nathalie's room at 4 a.m. on December 23rd what would that have felt like? She'd asked this in response to my saying that the experience in Nathalie's room was so much more real than anything that happened in the two days of funeral visitation, the funeral, the burial, etc.

I do realize the importance of rituals. I truly value them. The problem is that so much of what happens continues to create the illusion that death isn't cold, stark, empty of its threat. Death has no sting when one knows the truth of the experience I had in Nathalie's room.

January 2, 2000

What kind of experience did those people have who were in Nathalie's room after she died? How did they feel? Has the time spent there stayed with them? How? Are there any moments which stand out in their memory? Which ones? Did they learn anything from their time there? What? Questions, questions, questions.

I remember and still see, vividly, Nathalie's body lying on the bed. Eyes half open, only the whites showing, mouth gaping – empty – as if one were to come close and look inside they would see the bottom of the pit, the endless tunnel with nothing inside. Just a vessel which once held Nathalie's spirit and soul. I thought, Nathalie's essence is gone and what we'll bury in a few days is this container.

Where is she?

I would catch myself not wanting to look at the body. Yet in not looking I could see it clearly. My avoidance didn't wipe out the image. A picture of death is ever behind my eyes, etched like a fossil in time and just as permanent.

I felt free after two months of being cautious and careful of what I might say so as not to 'blow it'. I felt free to cry. No longer confronted by Nathalie's shaking index finger demanding, "Don't cry!" Free to speak of what this experience has meant to me. Free to be silent.

'O death where is thy sting?' Where does this quote come from? A poem perhaps?

It was a relief to see Germaine sitting at the head of Nathalie's bed gently stroking her arm as the body's warmth slowly wept away. Crying and shaking her head unable still to take in that her baby was dead.

When we spoke yesterday she said she had been restless on the 31st of December and finally asked Gerry to go to the cemetery. She didn't know if it helped. There is no grave marker. I asked her if she was glad, an odd word, she'd buried Nathalie's body rather than having it cremated. She immediately said, "Yes". There is a place she can go. A place she can tend, perhaps even plant something. A place she can bring flowers.

I recalled hearing a young mother whose child has died saying she went to the grave of her baby and wrapped it in a blanket against the winter's chill.

It was wonderful to be able to tell Germaine how lonely I felt in the house on New Year's Day 2000 with Guy in Quebec City. Germaine responded immediately, without hesitation, that I could come over anytime I wanted. Just to call to be sure they would be at home. God does answer prayers. Perhaps I'll go over today after I go to Colasanti's to do my two and one-half hours at the Master Gardeners' Advice Booth.

January 4, 2000

Gerry, Germaine, Martin and Chantal came over to the house to get Nathalie's obituaries. Darrin's mom had brought a laminating machine to their house. They were going to take back the newspaper clippings we had.

We all stood around in the kitchen talking for about 20 minutes before I asked them if they'd like to sit down! They talked back and forth for a bit deciding they could spare another 20 minutes.

It was so nice to see them again as it's nearly a week since the funeral. Actually a week today. Martin got enthralled with the Galileo thermometer I bought for Christmas for Guy placing his hands around it trying to get movement from the little discs inside. When Germaine added the warmth of her hands the discs actually began to move. Marty kept saying over and over that he wanted one.

Seated in the living room, Germaine looked closely at the basket she'd given me from amongst the many floral arrangements. She seemed to especially admire the *Dracena marginata* and the Azalea. She asked me if I put the Azalea outside in the spring could she have a cutting. "Yes", I said. I need to find out what kind of Azalea it is and if, in fact, it can go outside or if once it's bloomed it is as good as finished as a plant. I felt I could see regret in Germaine's eyes that she hadn't taken this particular plant home with her.

Gerry stayed in the background during our time together.

When they left I imagined that Marty looked into my eyes with an appreciation for my support of him.

I've decided to crochet the Noah's Ark afghan for Chantal's new baby. Germaine's and Gerry's first grandchild. When my youngest grandson, Brandon, is two and goes into a futon I'll make him a log cabin afghan just like Matthew's, his older brother. I'll just make Brandon's afghan in different colours.

Guy called to tell me he'd checked himself into the infirmary at Jam de Neiges hoping he'd get some rest. He doesn't rest deeply because it's too noisy where he sleeps. I wish he'd come home earlier than Friday so he'll have a few more days to recuperate. I've stopped saying anything as it doesn't change a thing. It might just make him 'dig in his heels'. He went to see his Aunt Rita and she made him his favourite supper, medium rare inside round steak, peas, mashed potatoes with gravy. I think he did his laundry while he was visiting. He sounds like he's got a cold. I have a terrible fear he'll come home and get really sick.

January 15, 2000

Guy and I went to the cemetery yesterday for the first time since Nathalie was buried. Her grave is marked with a small gray-edged marker with her name, date of death and plot number written on it. The flowers were lying over the top of the grave like an antique shawl.

Germaine isn't sleeping very well and not for a very long stretch of time. The house is empty, cold and strangely unkempt. Dead flowers and greenery are everywhere. Our arrangement now has Bells of Ireland which are more brown than green. They are also desiccated. The Protea has slumped to its knees like a penitent confessing his sins. The Gerberas have separated. Their petals lying dead like bugs after a warm June storm. Only the cedar branches and berries bear any resemblance to their former glory. The pine green votive candle is burning.

A candle is burning whenever Germaine is in the house.

She shows us a list of people who have donated money in Nathalie's memory. The page is filled on both sides with tiny checkmarks beside each entry. The dining room table is covered with papers making it look as if Germaine has been hard at work doing the tasks that accompany death. In fact she says she has just finished taking down the Christmas tree today. She'll tackle the thank you notes next.

Germaine and Gerry have ordered the marker – head stone – for Nathalie's grave. It will be grey with white lettering. It turns out they purchased a plot to hold the three of them. All three names with dates of birth, praying hands, flowers and a cross. Gerry's name is first to the far left; Nathalie is in the middle and Germaine on the far right.

The cost of death is very high.

I had thought perhaps Guy and I might buy a plot for ourselves in the same cemetery but as it turns out only parishioners of St. Anne's can be buried there.

February 13, 2000

How long since I've written? A long time. A month?

Since January 16th we've visited Germaine and Gerry several times including a time when Micheline came down for a few days. We went over last night after Guy came home from mass and stayed until 9 o'clock. Germaine has finished sending out all the thank you cards. She is still receiving the odd donation or card even now. She has also had some visits from two of Nathalie's friends who hadn't realized she was dead. In fact just the other night the phone rang quite late and the caller asked for Nathalie. Marty had answered the telephone. He was taken by surprise. So was the caller who immediately began to cry.

Germaine is sleeping about five hours, from 11 p.m. to 4

a.m. She gets up then, eats a bowl of cereal and goes back to bed. Sometimes. She is slowly finding the energy to clean the house. She helped Darrin's mom who, along with Micheline, made the invitations for Chantal's baby shower on February 26th. I doubt I'll have the afghan 'Noah's Ark' finished in time. Sometimes I even wonder if I'm meant to give it to Chantal at all. I'll wait and see I guess. Is this why I'm taking my time finishing it? If I push I'll have it done on time. I've asked Germaine twice now if it helps to talk about Nathalie and her YES is very firm. She worries people will get sick of her talking about her daughter.

I assure her I won't.

I'm still not sure when to tell her about this writing but I feel now it might actually help her to know and perhaps she can contribute to it?

Gerry and Marty seem to be denying their grief. Gerry does what comforts him. He watches television. Germaine says she'd like to get away for a couple of days with Gerry but she didn't sound hopeful. Marty doesn't have a job and he and his father sometimes don't see eye to eye.

Rob has been over to see Germaine and Gerry. Germaine took him downstairs to go through pictures and he took some to reproduce on his computer. I miss him and Charlotte. Perhaps I'll go to their church sometime.

EPILOGUE

So much has happened since I finished writing "In Her Room" on February 13, 2000.

Chantal and Darrin welcomed a beautiful baby boy in April, 2000. They named him Daniel. He has brought joy to them and to his grandparents. Germaine often cares for him while Chantal works. He is an active little fellow, curious and adventuresome as toddlers are when they feel cocooned in love.

Marty is working in Ottawa and living in Gatineau, Quebec.

Rob, the blue-eyed Celt, is working on his Master's in Biology at the University of Windsor. I invited Rob to sit with me and talk about his experience with Nathalie throughout the final months of her life. He decided not to and though I'm disappointed I respect his decision.

The pink and white Azalea that bloomed for over two years without a rest has stopped blooming.

I never returned to the Atrium to study.

The doctors did not advise Germaine or Gerry to make funeral arrangements before Nat died.

You may think that I was hard on the doctors and nurses who cared for Nathalie during her final illness. In hindsight I believe my blaming was a part of my grieving process. They were a close and convenient target for my anger and pain. In fact, the medical staff responsible for Nathalie's care were exemplary. I have nothing but admiration for each one of them. Early in 2000 there was a piece in the paper which said that during the time Nathalie was ill the hospital was in a crisis so serious a Code Orange was nearly put into effect. I was stunned when I read this. The concern and affection given to Nathalie and Germaine gave no indication of the gravity of their situation.

My piece on Art Roth's garden was published by *The Windsor Star* in early January. It was a full page spread on the front page of the Homes Section. Art had provided pictures showing the principal and some of the students working in the school garden.

On December 24, 2001, my darling Guy was diagnosed with cancer for the second time. Our lives have been like riding a roller coaster out of control ever since. Living with cancer is forcing us whether we like it or not to live one day at a time. To delight in the small things; the touch of his hand, a kiss lightly brushed across my lips, a look of love shining from his eyes. My warming his favourite afghan in the dryer on high heat before wrapping his thin body within its folds. My massaging his cold feet and toes before changing his socks every night. Preparing the pineapple and orange for his fruit salad each morning or cooking him two slices of crispy bacon, a scrambled egg sprinkled with cheese, a cup of decaf coffee and 60% whole wheat toast at our family physician's direction.

Holding hands as we lay side by side in bed each night. Sharing our fears and expressing our hopes in the wee hours of each morning's darkness.

I've learned something I thought I'd never learn. I am capable of giving love. I have learned I am capable of giving unconditional love. Not always. I am, after all, a human being. I've learned to put someone else's needs before my own desires. Not always. But enough times to know this sad process is changing me fundamentally.

Guy is recovering from the cancer but the prognosis is uncertain. Like Oprah says, one thing I know for sure: whatever happens our married life has been about deepening our spiritual growth, individually and as a couple. We are grateful for every thing that's happened throughout our 26 years together as husband and wife. All of it. The suffering and the joy. For it is true that I can't know one without experiencing the other.

My relationship with my daughter is still estranged. I wish I could tell you that everything is healed and that nothing is left unresolved. It would not be the truth. My prayer is that healing will take place in God's time. My daughter walks a spiritual path unique to her and separate from mine. Though I gave birth to her I do not own her. She is not mine. She is a gift. The pain which accompanies our journey is balanced by remembrances of laughter which made my stomach ache and which only she was capable of producing in me. Memories of beautiful flower arrangements brought to my door for every occasion – Mother's Day, Easter, Christmas, my birthday. Each one carefully orchestrated by my daughter's gifted artistic sense. Because she lived out of town and couldn't create the arrangements personally she would call a local florist and tell them in precise detail exactly what she had in mind and that she'd not tolerate anything less than the best.

I can see the beautiful casket spray for her Grandfather's funeral in '92, created from dozens of vermilion roses. How she tolerated my continually checking it to ensure the flowers remained fresh throughout the funeral visitation. Her impatience reined in by grief at my father's death. I remember the flowers she'd had for her second marriage in November 1990. The fragrance of the lilies linger in the air just a whisper away. I can see Guy walking her down the aisle. I can see myself arm-in-arm with a son on either side preceding my beautiful daughter.

The journal contains the sorrow I feel as a mother whose daughter doesn't want her in her life. I vacillate between sadness, anger, resignation and acceptance. I try not to give up hope that one day we'll be laughing together again. That one day the telephone will ring and her distinctive voice will say, "Am I speaking to 'Dr.' Jolin?" The voice barely able to contain the laughter bubbling beneath the surface, knowing how much delight she gives to me simply by being herself.

I don't claim to understand any of life's mysteries. I think we human beings are very brave choosing to incarnate knowing all the time that the Buddha was right – Life IS Suffering!

But, oh, can't life be marvelous? So full of joy, even moments of ecstasy.

I look forward to the day I am asked by St. Peter at the Pearly Gates, "Well Joannie, was it worth it?"

I hope my response will be a resounding "Yes"!

I hope the same for you.

I haven't been to Charlotte's church but she shared the following with me just days before I gave this manuscript to my publisher.

Throughout Nathalie's illness Charlotte had prayed the Angelus every day at noon hour. The Angelus is a prayer to our Blessed Mother. During Nathalie's burial service, the bells from St. Anne's Church began to ring out the 12 hours. The bells didn't ring out the 12 hours only, they rang in jubilation over and over again. Charlotte felt a shiver go through her body. She knew at that moment that her prayers had been answered. Our Lady was sending a message directly to her.

Nathalie is home for Christmas.

The following essays were written by Rob's younger brothers:

Nathalie

Nathalie was a very kind person. She and Rob took us swimming one time at her sister's house. It was fun. We also went tobogganing, and that was fun too!

I mostly remember that Nathalie was always happy. I never really saw her when she was sad.

We were all very very shocked and sad when we found out Nathalie was sick, and going to die. We went to Nathalie's graduation at the hospital. She looked very sick, but she seemed really happy.

When we went to Nathalie's funeral mass the church was completely full!!!! There must have been a lot of friends and family of Nathalie there. I also remember the church bells ringing. The mass was beautiful.

It was a very cold and dreary day. It was snowing. At the gravesite it was extremely cold! There were a lot of people at the gravesite. Rob was one of the last people standing outside. He must have been really cold. I felt sorry for him.

I'll miss Nathalie. She was a friend to many. I'll always remember her.

Alex
13 years old

Nathalie

I had this friend named Nathalie and she was very dear to me. When she got cancer it was sad but she got better. She always took me and Alex places such as swimming, bowling and lots of other places. When she got cancer again near Christmas of 1999 it was back to being worried. When we were told she wasn't going to make it to Christmas we were devastated. Then she finally went 3 days before Christmas. My brother Rob and boyfriend to Nathalie were very sad. It was almost worst seeing Rob this way than Nathalie's' death.

It was the day of the funeral that Rob was the worst. As Nathalie's coffin was being lowered into the hole Rob was yet again devastated. Me and my dad had a cold so we couldn't go out into the winter's cold.

May Nathalie rest in peace.

Andrew

11 years old

About the Author

Joan M. R. Jolin, B.S.W. was educated at the University of Western Ontario, King's College School of Social Work, London, Ontario, graduating in 1983. She has explored the areas of death and dying through a variety of venues including attending workshops with Elisabeth Kubler-Ross, M.D. and Dr. Gregg Furth, a Jungian analyst. Joan took a course in her second year at King's in Thanantology. Her professor was Dr. John 'Jack' Morgan, a pioneer in the field of death and dying. Joan has also read extensively on the subject and includes suggested references throughout the journal.

Joan, a former President of the Board of Directors, St. Leonard's House, Windsor worked for fifteen years in private practice with adult survivors of childhood sexual abuse before retiring in 1998 to devote her time to writing. She is currently a member of the Windsor and Essex County Master Gardeners group and The Ambassador Horticultural Society and has been published a number of times, most recently in the Windsor Star's *Master Gardener column. In Her Room is Joan's first work of length. She is presently at work on a book about addiction.*

Joan lives in Windsor, Ontario with her husband, Guy. They have three adult children, Greg, Lynda and Blake as well as eight grandchildren, Jennifer, Jeremiah, Melissa, Courtney, Benjamin, Janina, Matthew and Brandon.

MEMBER OF SCABRINI MEDIA

Quebec, Canada
2002